good dog

MODERN TRAINING METHODS

good dog

MODERN TRAINING METHODS

NEW HOLLAND

DR QUIXI SONNTAG

First published in 2007 by
New Holland Publishers
London • Cape Town • Sydney • Auckland
www.newhollandpublishers.com

Garfield House
86–88 Edgware Rd
London W2 2EA
United Kingdom

80 McKenzie Street
Cape Town 8001
South Africa

218 Lake Road
Northcote, Auckland
New Zealand

14 Aquatic Drive
Frenchs Forest,
NSW 2086
Australia

Publishing managers: Claudia Dos Santos, Simon Pooley
Commissioning editor: Alfred LeMaitre
Editors: Alfred LeMaitre and Ruth Hamilton
Concept Design: Christelle Marais
Designer: Pete Bosman
Illustrator: Steven Felmore
Production: Marion Storz
Consultant: Mary Martin

ISBN: 978 184537 176 0

Reproduction by Pica Digital PTE Ltd, Singapore
Printed and bound by Star Standard Industries PTE Ltd, Singapore

10 9 8 7 6 5 4 3 2 1

Contents

Introduction

DOGS ADD VALUE TO PEOPLE'S LIVES IN MANY different ways. They are loyal companions, entertainers and protectors. They make us feel wanted, relieve our depression and provide physical comfort. For many people, the relationship with their dog is as important as any human relationship. While dogs play a major role in promoting our quality of life, our relationship with dogs can sometimes have negative effects. And when a dog's behaviour negatively affects our quality of life, it often brings the relationship to an end.

Sadly, behavioural and training problems are a common reason for the relinquishment of dogs. For many people, a dog's behaviour problem can have such a negative impact on their lives that they feel they have no choice but to give up the dog. Unfortunately, the majority of dogs relinquished in these circumstances end up being euthanased. It is sad and most disconcerting that so many otherwise healthy dogs are sacrificed as a direct result of behavioural problems, usually in the prime of their lives, at around two years of age. What makes it particularly tragic is that most behavioural problems are not only treatable, but also preventable.

Most are the result of misunderstandings and miscommunication between people and dogs. By understanding our dogs better – what they really need, how they really think – we can become more skilled and successful dog managers. If we can learn to think more like dogs, if we can see the world through their eyes, we will be able to foresee problems and intervene timeously and appropriately.

Managing dogs requires a holistic approach. We must consider their physical and mental well-being, emotional and social needs, and environmental and cognitive enrichment. Training a dog is about much more than getting it to do things on command. It is about communicating your needs and allowing your dog to communicate his. It is about understanding what your dog is trying to say. Dog training can only work if we understand what makes dogs do things, and how they communicate their needs.

Understanding canine body language and emotions is central to successful training. Similarly, knowing how dogs learn enables us to look deeper into their psyches. Training provides mental stimulation as well as structured social interaction for the dog, both of which are essential for his, and your, happiness.

Opposite *Training provides mental and physical stimulation.*

Traditional dog training was human-centred, and aimed to teach dogs to accomplish behaviours that are useful for humans. But it neglected to teach them things that might be to their own advantage, such as social and relaxation skills. Often, apparently highly trained dogs show signs of severe anxiety, which begs the question: are they really enjoying training?

Dog training is about building up a special rapport between human and canine so that their quality of life is enhanced. It is not about

Above Dog training can only be successful if all a dog's needs are satisfied.

winning the next obedience competition. By creating a clear channel of communication with our dogs, we can help them to develop skills that will ensure they cope well with all the stresses we and our world impose on them. Training is really teaching – sharing with our dogs the ways in which we can enjoy each other's company.

You don't have to join a dog training school to enjoy all the benefits of training – home training as described in this book can be even more beneficial. If, in so doing, you do develop the skills required for obedience and other competitions, and if you enjoy the competitive dog-sport arena, nothing stops you from participating – as long as it is about promoting your dog's well-being and not your self-image.

The biggest benefit of dog training is that it enables us to make a closer connection with our dogs, thereby making it easier to recognize, understand and address any problems they may have, or may develop.

Among other things, training gives us the opportunity to teach our dogs good social skills, so that we can live together in harmony and enjoy each other's company. It also makes it possible to teach our dogs different behaviours that have functional or entertainment value. Training provides us with the opportunity to enjoy quality time together, thus making life better for all, dogs and humans.

If this book helps to bring you and your dog closer together, then it has accomplished its goal. Learn as much as you can about your dog and dogs in general so that you can become a better teacher yourself!

Above *Breed showing, as other competitive dog activities, can be rewarding for both dog and owner, provided it is done for the right reasons.*

Chapter **1**

The origins of dogs

SCIENTIFIC EVIDENCE CONFIRMS THAT DOGS (*Canis familiaris*) evolved from wolves (*Canis lupus*) between 130,000 and 14,000 years ago. How the process of domestication took place remains a mystery. Why did some wolves become dogs, and others not? Did people need dogs, or did dogs need people? Do dogs and humans get along simply because they like each other? Several theories exist.

Whatever the answer may be, the domestic dog has been a constant human companion for a very long time. Over the centuries, it has been used and abused in many different ways. Today's dogs are not only the product of their wolf ancestors, but also that of highly selective breeding orchestrated by people.

The development of breeds

From 12 distinguishable dog types in Roman times, we today have more than 400 recognized dog breeds worldwide. No other species exhibits such a wide range of physical and behavioural characteristics – from the tiny but feisty Yorkshire terrier to the huge, fun-loving Newfoundland. It is only in the last 100–150 years that breeds as we know them have started appearing.

Most of the dog breeds we are familiar with today originated from a mixture of other breeds, and the majority of these have very little in common with their modern counterparts. As dog breeding became a popular business, more breed characteristics developed as a direct result of human whims, rather than necessity.

The original breeds were all bred with a specific purpose in mind. Hunting was a popular pursuit in the Middle Ages, and dogs were bred with a focus on specific aspects of the hunt; some specialized in tracking (scent hounds), others in chasing (sight hounds), and others were utilized specifically for pointing (finding prey and identifying its location) or retrieving (gundogs). Guarding and fighting were also traits that were specifically selected in certain breeds.

Today, most dogs are companions. Though they are still sometimes used for their original purpose, very few dog owners nowadays seriously participate in the activities that the dogs were engaged in as little as a century ago. Nevertheless, what dogs are today has a lot to do with the traits selected by breeders over the past few hundred years.

Opposite *The wolf* (Canis lupus) *is the common ancestor of all modern dog breeds.*

Knowing what a certain breed was bred for can help create a better understanding of an individual dog's behaviour and looks. Indeed, many of the physical and behavioural eccentricities of breeds become clearer once you learn more about their history.

The wolf in your dog

How much wolf is there in the 21st-century dog? Comparing dogs to wolves has a certain romantic appeal: people like to think of their pet dog as a tame wolf, wild and mysterious and providing a direct link to nature. This romantic notion has some truth in that there are certain similarities between dogs and wolves. Today's dogs still have a perception of social life that reflects the wolf pack system, and many of their habits, such as digging holes and using urine and faeces to mark their territory, are similar to those of wolves.

However, there are also many differences, and we should not attribute everything a dog does to some lupine characteristic.

The social life of wolves

Let us consider the social behaviour of wolves, and how it does or does not relate to dogs. According to the pack theory, higher-ranking animals in a group have higher social status and, as a result, they are entitled to privileged access to the resources that are shared by the group. (Social status refers to the ability of an animal to gain access to valuable resources. The animal that controls the most resources has the highest social status.) The more variation in social status among the members of a group, the less conflict there is among them. The social hierarchy therefore promotes harmony within the group, and its survival.

In wolves, aggressive interaction to determine contested social ranking is usually limited to displays of dominance between two individuals, until one submits. Real fights are reserved for the individuals from outside the group who threaten its safety. Dominance and submission are displayed through an elaborate set of visual signals using various aspects of body language such as movement of the lips, ears and tail, and using posture and facial expression to communicate either submission or dominance. Only if a conflict cannot be resolved with body language displays will a fight ensue.

Left Wolves are social animals that live in groups.

Wolf packs have strong leaders that take the lead in most important activities such as hunting and breeding. Strong leadership promotes security and coherence within the pack. The pack leader is usually referred to as the alpha wolf. Males and females have parallel, separate hierarchies, each with an alpha animal occupying the highest position. The existence of a hierarchy and the development of a highly refined visual communication system (body language) to address conflict are examples of how wolves have adapted to group living.

The social life of dogs

Although some aspects of wolf social structure apply to dogs as well, we should take care not to equate the two. They are not the same and do not share the same type of environment. Incorrect interpretations of how wolves' social structure applies to dogs have led to many misunderstandings.

Above: *Two dogs playfully vie for control over a bone.*

Social hierarchy among dogs is evident in most multidog households, as anyone who owns more than one dog will agree. There is often a clear distinction between two dogs in that the submissive one always yields to the more assertive one – for example, by giving up bones, toys, attention and even food. However, in many cases this distinction is not at all clear, often when there is a lot of overt aggression between dogs (see Chapter 9).

What is the role of people in the social system? Do dogs perceive them as part of their social system? Is it important that people act like pack leaders? The answer to all these questions is a qualified yes. Dogs do see people as part of their social system, and the way people behave around them affects dogs profoundly.

Remarkable changes in canine behaviour can be brought about by small changes in human behaviour. The role of humans as pack leaders is where the real controversy lies. Dogs do have an inherent need to fit into a social system where humans offer effective leadership. However, this leadership is less about social status than it is about providing consistent rule structure and appropriate social interaction. The latter means providing the dog with structured opportunities for social interaction and not reinforcing inappropriate or attention-seeking behaviour.

There is no doubt that consistency and appropriate social interaction help dogs feel emotionally secure and make them easier to control. One theory that explains why this is so is the resource management theory described in Chapter 4, which provides practical tips on how to produce a predictable environment in which your dog feels safe. If you can learn to be a competent resource manager, your dog will trust you and defer to you willingly.

Above *Controlling an energetic dog requires consistent rewards for good behaviour, rather than physical force.*

The dominance myth

Have you ever been told to show your dog that you are dominant, or been advised to alpha roll your puppy, forcing him onto his back and growling into his face? Have you been told that it is fine to scruff your puppy when he urinates in the house, and to rub his nose in the mess? Or that you should shake your dog when she doesn't respond to your commands, or use a choke-chain or spike-collar if she doesn't want to walk next to you on the lead?

This type of advice to dog owners is based on a complete misinterpretation of the social status of dogs and the concept of 'dominance', thinking that the use of physical force is the type of leadership dogs need.

Physical force does not show your dog that you are in control, but that you resort to force because you are not a competent resource manager. If you manage resources effectively your dog will respect you and you will not need to use force. Advocates of physical force justify the use of alpha rolls and scruffing because 'they are methods that wolves use to discipline each other, especially their young'. This notion is incorrect. A weaker wolf submits willingly, while the assertive one will stand over the submitting wolf to reinforce its status. Likewise, scruffing is not a method wolves use to discipline each other, but in serious fights (usually among individuals from different packs) with the intention of causing severe damage. The only type of discipline that takes place between adults and young is the muzzle hold, an inhibited bite over the muzzle of the cub. Adult wolves are surprisingly tolerant of cubs and very rarely discipline their young.

We are not wolves, neither are our dogs. And even if there was any value in acting like wolves it is doubtful whether we would ever make good enough impersonations to convince our dogs anyway.

Aggression and dominance

Dogs interpret scruffing, alpha rolls and other types of force as forms of aggression. They will first try to avoid the conflict by being appeasing (showing deference, for example, by looking away, holding their tail between their legs or urinating), and if that doesn't work they will respond by defending themselves by growling and then biting. Young dogs that are treated with force become fearful, and this fear can later turn into aggression, not only towards the person doing the disciplining, but with any person who approaches them. Remember that aggression breeds aggression.

Aggression and dominance are often used interchangeably, but incorrectly. This is partly why so many people think that, in order to show their dog leadership, they must use force. Many canine behaviourists prefer not to use the term dominance at all, and instead refer to assertive or status-related behaviour. Aggression is defined as a threat or challenge that is ultimately resolved by combat or deference. Dominance is defined as priority access to a preferred resource and refers to a social relationship between two dogs. The whole point of dominance and submission in a social hierarchy is to avoid aggression, which will only ensue if another dog challenges access to a given resource and submission does not resolve it.

Above *Dogs can be well trained without owners ever resorting to aggression or punishment.*

> *You do not need aggression to discipline a dog*

Your dog will perceive you to be dominant when you feed him and take his food away (you are in control of the food resource, see Chapter 4). You will have dominance because you are consistent in applying rules, like no begging at the table. Your dog will

perceive you to be dominant if you control access to his toys by keeping some out of reach and handing them out selectively. Aggression is not required in any of these situations.

The importance of family

The social structure in a dog's life revolves around the dogs and people with whom she lives. They make up her group or pack and they are the ones she will relate to on a daily basis.

Dogs do not perceive unfamiliar people and dogs as being part of their social system. Many find them threatening or dangerous, and do not trust them. A dog that is unsure of strange people, will, for example, feel threatened by direct eye contact from someone he doesn't know, whereas direct eye contact from his owner may help him feel more secure. If a dog gets clear leadership signals from his owner he may find it easier to cope with unfamiliar people and dogs because he is more likely to take the lead from the owner in a stressful

Above The people and animals that a dog relates to on a daily basis make up his social structure.

situation. Different treatment strategies are necessary for dogs that show aggression to strangers, as opposed to dogs that are aggressive towards their owners.

Ideally, dogs should be socialized with people and dogs outside their own social group or family from a very young age (two to three months) so that they become used to dealing with the unknown.

In the first few months, their experiences with people and dogs should always be pleasant to ensure that they make positive associations. If, as young puppies, they have the opportunity to get to know people and other dogs in a friendly environment, they will be less likely to develop problems with strange people or other dogs as they mature.

How dogs communicate

Visual signals

Dogs have a repertoire of visual signals or body language that they use to communicate with each other, although it is not as elaborate as that of wolves. The physical characteristics of some dogs prohibit the use of meaningful visual signals: droopy ears and curly or docked tails are less effective for communication than pricked ears and long tails. Likewise, long-coated dogs cannot raise their hackles when they feel threatened. (Read more about canine body language in Chapter 5.)

Pheromones

Pheromones are chemicals that animals use to communicate with each other by means of smell. The young of many species can recognize and locate their mothers through pheromones, which also play an important part in reproduction because they attract individuals to one another. Dogs excrete pheromones in their faeces, urine and anal-sac content. (Dogs often urinate on another dog's urine as an expression of social status, territory marking, or simply to make their presence known.) Male dogs can detect a bitch in oestrus over large distances simply by the smell of her urine.

In recent years, research has focused on the use of pheromones in the treatment of behavioural disorders. A synthetically produced dog-appeasing pheromone (DAP) – an analogue of the pheromone that bitches produce from the patch of skin between their mammary glands – is now being used to treat various anxiety disorders in dogs.

Top *The anal sacs are situated on either side of the anus and produce pheromones. By smelling these, dogs get to know each other.*

Middle *Sniffing another dog's backside provides valuable social information.*

Above *This dog uses visual signals – ears back, open mouth displaying teeth – to communicate that she does not wish to interact aggressively.*

Above *Barking is usually an alert signal, but can also accompany fear or aggression.*

Vocalization

In young puppies, barking in the form of whimpering or whining is a distress signal and is often elicited by fear or excitement. Dogs often bark and howl in sympathy with other dogs, not necessarily to convey a message but to seek social contact. Different types of barks can indicate a dog's emotional state at a given time – deep, low-pitched barks are more likely to accompany aggression while a high-pitched scream may indicate intense fear or anxiety.

Growling often precedes biting, and should be seen as a warning that the dog perceives a threat and may react aggressively. In quite a different context, growling also often accompanies play.

How dogs perceive the world

Eyes and vision

Dogs certainly see the world differently to humans. They see poorly at very short distances, so something that is right in front of them will be blurred and out of focus. They use their sense of smell to locate objects that they cannot see. They also have limited 3D (binocular) vision, but possess a wider field of vision. In other words they can see further to the side due to the placement of the eyes in their skulls. Dogs have excellent night vision and can see well in dim light. Although they can distinguish colour, their colour vision is limited. They can also notice extremely subtle movements and have an uncanny ability to anticipate their owners' movements.

Dogs that are born blind or with poor vision usually learn to cope very well with their disability, especially if they remain in a familiar environment, but they are likely to have problems interacting with other dogs, as their own visual signalling and interpretation of other dogs' visual signals is impaired.

Ears and hearing

Dogs can hear sounds at a distance of 450m (1350ft) that humans can only discern at 100m (300ft). They also have the exceptional ability to identify the source of a sound, as their ability to move their ears helps with sound localization.

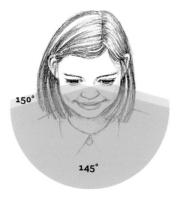

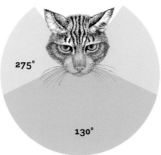

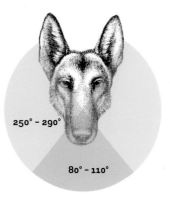

A human sees from side-to-side a total of 150°, of which 145° is binocular overlap.

A cat sees from side-to-side a total of 275°, of which 130° is binocular overlap.

A dog has a total vision of 250–290°, with 80–110° of overlap – much less than that of humans.

Dogs can hear sounds of much higher frequency than humans – up to 60kHz (sounds within the ultrasonic range), as opposed to 20kHz for people. It is likely that this is useful in hunting, as small rodents make high-pitched sounds within this range. Although all dogs are sensitive to very loud noises, some breeds, such as the border collie, seem to be especially sound sensitive. The herding breeds, in general, appear to be more susceptible to noise phobias than most other breeds.

The world of smells

The part of the brain responsible for processing smells is far larger in dogs than in humans. Nerves that come from this area in the brain are directly connected to the mucous lining of the nose. The nasal lining (mucosa) of the dog is considerably larger and more sensitive in detecting smells than that of humans. Dogs have 220 million scent receptors in 700 sq cm (276 sq in) of nasal mucosa, while people only have 5 million scent receptors in 50 sq cm (20 sq in) of nasal mucosa.

Not only do dogs have the ability to detect tiny wafts of smell (some can identify a one-month-old human scent from a fingerprint on a glass pane), but their ability to identify one particular scent from a multitude of others in the environment is particularly impressive. For this reason, they are used worldwide to sniff out drugs, explosives, people trapped in disaster zones, missing children and poison.

Dogs use their sense of smell to find out more about their environment, just as we would use our eyes to read or observe in order to gain information. To them, being able to sniff different interesting smells while out on a walk is probably as much a part of the fun as the physical exercise.

Canine life stages

The important first four months

The first four months of a puppy's life are extremely important in terms of his or her future behaviour. Starting at three weeks, puppies learn about their environment through investigative behaviour and social interactions. What they learn at this sensitive period of their lives will stay with them forever. This is the time when puppies are most receptive to new environmental stimuli – after four months they become more apprehensive of the unknown and are more likely to respond with fear to novel situations and impressions.

If a puppy's interactions and encounters during these first months are varied and positive, it is more likely that he will be confident and relaxed when he is exposed to new things later in life. Provided they are pleasant, all of the puppy's first experiences will have positive connotations as he grows up: riding in a car, people with hats, things on wheels, umbrellas, children and various household sounds.

***Above** Puppies that are exposed to new things early in life are more likely to accept such stimuli later in their lives.*

Puppies are very keen learners. You should start training your puppy as early as possible, from 8 to 10 weeks. The sooner puppies learn what constitutes appropriate behaviour the less likely they are to develop problematic habits. Training methods that make use of positive reinforcement are extremely effective in teaching dogs of all ages the basics of good manners.

Challenges for the owners of young puppies include house-training, managing their destructive behaviour, controlling the intensity of their play and teaching the puppy not to nip and chew people (bite inhibition).

The most common physical problem in young puppies is gastroenteritis, often caused by their propensity for ingesting inedible objects. Puppies between two and four months also need regular vaccinations and deworming.

The adolescent stage – 5 to 18 months

Many owners report a definite change in their puppy's behaviour from about five months. She focuses less on them, is more interested in what is going on around her and appears to have forgotten all her training.

The best way to deal with this is to accept it and resolve to be extremely patient and consistent. Stick to your rules – the puppy still loves you, and certainly should not be spoiled at this stage. She has simply discovered some things that are temporarily far more interesting than you are. Maintain your puppy's interest by being the only source of valuable resources such as food, treats, toys and cuddles (see Chapter 4). Do not give her anything she considers valuable unless she has carried out an instruction from you such as to sit or lie down. She needs consistency from you to carry her through this phase.

Have short but frequent and interesting training sessions, and expect not to achieve a high level of training when she is at her peak of disinterest. By about a year of age (sometimes later), most puppies have gained some dignity and become willing learners again.

During the four-to-six-month period, puppies grow extremely fast. They may look quite gangly and thin at this stage, and often have inordinately huge appetites. (Be careful to adjust the diet when their growth slows down again.) This is also the period during which they lose their milk teeth. Teething often coincides with a period of renewed destructiveness that can be linked to discomfort, but boredom is a common cause of destructive behaviour at this age and can be prevented by providing physical and mental stimulation in the form of walks, training, food-dispensing toys and chews (see Chapter 3).

Separation-related problems can begin during the first year of a puppy's life, or later. Puppies need to learn how to be alone and content. In some cases there is a true separation anxiety, and you may need to address this with a combination of behaviour-modification techniques and medication.

Above *During the adolescent stage, puppies need lots of physical and mental stimulation.*

Between 6 and 12 months, dogs reach puberty. Bitches come on heat approximately every six months unless they are spayed. This is also the time when young dogs often develop 'growth pains'. In many instances these are just transient bouts of lameness, but sometimes they are symptomatic of serious joint problems that may require surgery, especially in large and giant breeds.

In the larger dog breeds, excessive weight-bearing exercise, overfeeding or providing feed that is too energy-dense, or is too rich in calcium, will exacerbate joint problems such as hip and elbow dysplasia. These juvenile dogs have different nutritional requirements than small-breed youngsters. Their specific needs are reflected in the commercial diets that are available in shops and at vet practices.

Social maturity – 18 to 36 months

At social maturity, challenges for social status become more apparent. This is the time when social hierarchy becomes an issue for most dogs. Certain types of dogs seem to be more concerned with their social status than others. As a result, aggression, both between dogs in the same household and between dogs and people, becomes prevalent at this age.

Social maturity is also the age at which several other behavioural disorders such as fears, phobias and compulsive disorders can become evident. Small-breed dogs stop growing at about 12 months, large and giant breeds at about 18 months. At this time they should switch from a puppy diet to a mature or maintenance diet. Dogs usually need less food now, as they have completed growing. So watch your dog's weight

Above *Irish Wolfhounds from l–r; an adult dog, a 2 month old puppy and a 5 month old teenager.*

carefully lest you overfeed it. Obesity is the most common dog nutritional problem in the developed world.

Through maturity into seniority – seven years plus

With the advent of highly specialized canine nutrition and the continuous advances in veterinary science, dogs are living longer; some can reach more than 15 years of age. A dog older than seven years is considered to be a senior canine. Small breeds tend to age slower and live longer than large breeds. Physical conditions related to seniority include

Above As dogs get older, they still benefit from training, but will be less physically active and will tire sooner.

heart and kidney failure, arthritis, tooth decay (this is best addressed preventatively by getting the young puppy used to having his teeth brushed regularly), blindness and deafness. Older dogs can also develop fears and phobias and can become the victims of interdog aggression as they become older and weaker, while younger dogs will challenge them and want to take over their position in the social hierarchy.

Chapter 2

How your dog thinks

As YOU EMBARK ON THE JOURNEY OF TEACHING your dog how to behave, you will benefit immensely from a clear understanding of how he thinks and learns. This will help you to communicate successfully with your dog, because he does not instinctively know how you want him to behave. When a dog appears not to be listening to you, it is usually due to a lack of effective communication on your part – you are not sending a clear enough message about what you expect from the dog.

Understanding the process that goes on in your dog's mind when he behaves in a certain manner will help you find effective ways of letting him know how you want him to behave so that you can both live in harmony.

Why dogs behave the way they do

Dogs do things because they are genetically programmed to react (instinctive behaviour), or because they have learned from experience to do something in a given context (learnt behaviour). In practice, most behaviour has both instinctive and learnt components.

Instinctive behaviour

Dogs do certain things instinctively, without any training whatsoever; their brains are hardwired to do them without thinking. Instinctive behaviour is something a dog is born with. Examples of instinctive behaviour are:

- Stalking and chasing small animals (predatory behaviour)
- Herding
- Eating food scraps (scavenging)
- In bitches: the biting off of the umbilical cord and eating the placenta
- Rolling in scents
- Burying bones

As dog owners, we must be aware of the instincts that drive our dogs, and use this knowledge to provide adequately for their needs. Some instincts are stronger in some breeds, and different breeds have different instincts. The stronger an instinct, the more difficult it is to modify with training.

You will never be able to suppress strong innate behaviour. Instead you should provide an environment in which your dog can safely express such a need. (Read more about fulfilling your dog's needs in Chapters 3 and 4.)

Learnt behaviour

Learnt behaviour is also known as acquired behaviour. Dogs learn from their experiences

Opposite *Golden retrievers have a very strong instinct for picking things up and bringing them back; thus they require little training to teach them to retrieve.*

Above *This exercise takes a lot of concentration and self-control, especially considering the golden retriever's natural love of food!*

and from the consequences of their actions. They acquire new behaviour through operant and classical conditioning (see pp30–33). Both principles are applied in dog training, but operant conditioning is what enables dogs to learn new skills.

The role of the canine brain in learning

The brain, the body's control centre, performs several functions. Simply put, the brain and its functions have three main parts. Firstly, there is the 'primitive' brain that regulates physiological activities in the body such as breathing, eating and heart function. These controls occur mainly in the brainstem, in the lower, rear part of the brain. Then there is the limbic system, the main site for processing emotions. The limbic system is situated in the centre of the brain and has many complex connections with the other parts of the brain. The most advanced part of the brain is the cerebral cortex, which helps the animal think and process thoughts and emotions. The cerebral cortex is situated in the outer part of the brain.

When a dog perceives a stimulus, the information is transmitted via nerves to the brain where it is processed. The dog will respond to the stimulus within a millisecond. If, for example, a dog sees a fast-moving object, the image is transmitted via the optic nerve to the area in the brain that processes visual stimuli. The brain is pre-programmed to recognize prey behaviour, and the dog responds by chasing the object. If the stimulus is not recognized as prey, the dog will respond in a different way, by barking, for example. How the stimulus is processed in the brain depends on the hard-

The canine brain

(transverse section)

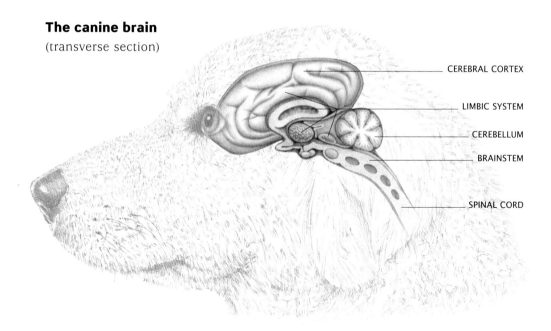

CEREBRAL CORTEX

LIMBIC SYSTEM

CEREBELLUM

BRAINSTEM

SPINAL CORD

wiring of the brain, namely the type of instinctive behaviour that is genetically programmed for that dog (certain dogs have a stronger predatory instinct than others, for example), and the dog's previous experiences. If a dog has learned from experience that a stimulus is dangerous, she may resort to running away. Three dogs may respond to the same stimulus in three different ways. An instinctive response is automatically processed in the limbic system and brainstem regions of the brain – the dog does not get a chance to think about its response.

A learned response, on the other hand, is processed in the cerebral cortex and involves conditioning. The dog has to make a decision about how to respond to a specific stimulus. For example, the owner holds out the dog's food bowl (stimulus). The dog immediately sits

(response), because she has learned that sitting in that context gives her access to the food.

The more we teach our dogs to think for themselves, the less likely they will be to react instinctively. Instinctive reactions often result in problems, because these reactions may not be appropriate in the given context. Trained behaviours become default behaviours, and the result is that your dog is more likely to offer default (well-trained) behaviour in situations of uncertainty. The more good behaviour you can teach your dog, the more likely he will be to act appropriately in situations where he has to figure out an apt response for himself.

Operant conditioning

Operant conditioning is when a dog decides to do something because she knows that it will have a positive consequence, or enable her to avoid a negative result. It is voluntary behaviour that depends on a known consequence, the reward. Operant conditioning is used to teach a dog good behaviour and also to deal with existing unwanted behaviour. In operant conditioning, animals learn by remembering the consequences of their actions.

Dogs do what works for them

Dogs learn that certain actions have positive consequences, while others do not. They will consciously choose to repeat those things that

have positive consequences and avoid doing those that elicit no response or a negative reaction. The positive consequence of a behaviour is called positive reinforcement. It is something a dog is willing to work for – a reward. Dogs do things because they are beneficial to them, not because they want to please us (though interacting with us is rewarding for them) or out of spite or to irritate us. They simply try out different things and repeat those actions that have a positive consequence.

The underlying principle of operant conditioning is that dogs do whatever is advantageous to them. Operant conditioning is how dogs learn new skills and how they can be trained to do specific things. (In Chapters 6 and 7 you will learn how to apply operant conditioning in training your dog to perform various behaviours.)

Dogs learn through trial and success

Dogs are much better at learning from positive results than from negative ones. Therefore the best way to teach a dog something is to ensure that you repeatedly reward what you want him to do until it has become conditioned (learnt).

Timing is everything

Dogs do what works for them, but they can only learn from the positive consequences of their actions if these consequences occur immediately – within one second – after the

Left *If you find something that really motivates your dog, you can train him successfully. This dog is willing to work for access to the toy.*

action. You must directly link the reward with the behaviour you are rewarding. The same applies to punishment (see p34), if you are ever to use it.

Food is usually an effective reward. Have food treats readily available in different locations by placing treat containers in various strategic places around the house, and practise giving a treat almost simultaneously with good behaviour. The use of a conditioned reinforcer, as in clicker training, makes it possible to be even more accurate with delivering the reward at exactly the right time.

Consciously look out for good behaviour in your dog – be observant, so that you don't miss out on good opportunities to reward it.

Dogs learn all the time

Dogs learn through constant interaction with their environment. They try out different things and, depending on the immediate consequence of an action, they will either do it again and again, or try something else.

Above *Recognise good behaviour and reward it, like this dog who remains calm and controlled while being touched by children.*

Your dog is learning every day and every hour, even when you are not around. Dogs can learn in a structured way through formal training sessions and informally, when neither you nor a trainer are actively involved. In Chapter 3 we discuss how you can create the ideal environment for effective learning, both structured and informal.

Successful behaviour is conditioned

Every time a dog initiates an activity and successfully completes it, the behaviour has been reinforced and the dog is more likely to repeat that activity in future. The more often he has

Examples of good behaviour

- Keeps all four paws on the ground when greeting people
- Comes when you call
- Sits quietly on his mat when you are eating
- Plays with his toy
- Relaxes while children pet him

the opportunity to perform a specific behaviour, the harder he'll try doing it in future. Successful execution of the behaviour can be rewarding in itself. This is why it is so important to actively avoid situations in which unwanted behaviour occurs if you want the dog to stop doing it.

Shaping

Shaping means building up a behaviour in tiny steps, by reinforcing many small improvements along the way. Put differently, shaping is changing an ordinary behaviour such as sitting into an extraordinary or advanced behaviour so that, for example, your dog sits well for several minutes while you walk away out of sight and other dogs walk past him.

When teaching your dog anything that does not come naturally, break it down into its smallest component and start from there. A paw lift, for example, could start off as a shift in weight onto one side, thereby only slightly lifting one paw off the ground. Once that comes naturally, you can start to increase the standard and only reinforce higher paw lifts. (See chapters 6 and 7 for practical shaping exercises.)

Classical conditioning

Classical conditioning, also referred to as respondent conditioning, is an involuntary response by the animal that takes place in the absence of reward. It refers to dogs learning about things that are not dependent on their own actions; in other words, reward and punishment

Above *Although the dog is expected to ultimately give a paw as in a handshake, this slight movement of the paw can be reinforced initially. After a while, only higher paw movements are reinforced, until a proper handshake is shaped.*

do not play a role here. It is about making associations between things that are not naturally associated with one another. Through classical conditioning, dogs learn to indirectly associate certain external things (environmental stimuli) with internal reactions, such as physiological reflexes or emotions.

The most famous example of classical conditioning is the experiments performed by the famous Russian scientist, Ivan Pavlov. He knew that it was a natural reflex for dogs to salivate when they were about to eat. He made sure that every time his dogs were fed, they would hear the sound of a bell ringing at the same time. Thus the bell, the food and the salivation (something the dog has no control over, as it is a body reflex) become associated with one another. After many repetitions, Pavlov wanted to see what would happen if he rang the bell without feeding the dogs, and found that they salivated even though there was no food present. The sound of the bell, which initially had no effect on the dogs, became conditioned to have the same effect as food. The dogs did not learn to salivate consciously – their brain simply made the association between the bell and the food until the bell meant 'food' to the dogs.

Fear and classical conditioning

Classical conditioning of fear is common in dogs. A dog may have been happy to interact with children for a number of years until a balloon popped right next to him during an

otherwise positive interaction with a child. From then on he has a fear of children. A puppy that is stung by a bee as he discovers a new toy may exhibit a fear of similar toys thereafter.

Any negative experience that causes fear will affect a dog's future behaviour if he associates the fear with something else that happens to be in the environment at the same time.

Practical application

Getting a dog used to new and possibly intimidating situations and experiences, and changing an existing fearful or otherwise negative response to a positive one, requires classical conditioning. The latter is referred to as desensitisation and counter-conditioning (see Chapter 9) and is often used in the treatment of anxiety and phobias. These processes are often employed in conjunction with operant conditioning.

Right Drooling (salivation) in anticipation of a tasty treat.

Punishment

Why punishment doesn't work

Punishment can range from mild to highly aversive. What is mild for one dog may be highly aversive to another. What you consider to be mild may not be perceived the same way by your dog. Punishment that causes any level of discomfort, pain or fear is unnecessary and unacceptable. Severe forms of punishment, such as choking, shock collars and beatings, are abusive and most definitely do not have a place in dog training.

The biggest problem with punishment is that by merely stopping problem behaviour we are not giving the dog any clues about what we do expect from him. Punishment does not tell the dog anything about good behaviour. It is only through positive reinforcement that we can tell the dog what we do expect.

Punishment is difficult to apply correctly

If punishment was really effective, it should only have to be used once or twice in a given situation. The main reasons that punishment is so often ineffective are as follows:

- **Timing:** Unless punishment is delivered within a second of the unwanted behaviour, it will not work. Dogs only learn from the immediate consequences of their actions. We are usually late with punishment and teach the dog something that is not clearly linked to their behaviour. An example is punishing a dog that runs out of the gate, only when he eventually returns. The dog learns that coming back, not running away, has negative consequences.

- **Intensity:** If punishment is too mild, the dog soon becomes used to it and it loses meaning. However, punishment that is too severe causes fear. Fear is not conducive to effective learning. Different dogs, and the same dog in different situations, require different levels of punishment. There is no

Left The shake can (a tin containing some coins, nails or screws) or water spray are mild aversive stimuli that can be used to interrupt unwanted behaviour before the dog is redirected to acceptable behaviour.

simple method for determining and measuring the appropriate severity of punishment in each situation.

- **Context:** Punishment should be associated only with the punished behaviour. Dogs usually associate punishment with other things, like the person punishing them or a particular location, not their behaviour. If you punish your dog every time you see him doing something wrong, he may just learn not to do it in your presence. Puppies that are punished for messing in the house typically learn to hide behind the couch to go, instead of learning where it is appropriate to do their business.

Above Use a time-out in a boring place, rather than punishment, if your dog is misbehaving.

Alternatives to punishment

To distract a dog that is about to engage in an undesirable activity, you could consider using a shake can containing bits of metal or coins that make a noise, or a spray from a water bottle (with or without a few drops of citronella oil). Do not use these interrupters if your dog reacts with more than a mild startle. Interruption techniques are discussed in greater detail in Chapter 8.

Withholding reward is a very powerful tool for the dog trainer. Environmental and social rewards can often be manipulated (see p40). Be consistent when giving treats and attention to your dog and only do it when he is well-behaved.

A specific form of withholding positive reinforcement is the time-out. This means placing the dog in a situation that is less reinforcing than the preceding situation. Ideally, it should be an environment with little stimulation or interest, such as an enclosed courtyard or the bathroom. The dog is moved from a stimulating, reinforcing environment to a very boring environment as soon as he behaves inappropriately. To be effective, the dog must find the time-out environment less appealing than the

Above Dogs show submissive behaviour in response to a social cue, not because they feel guilty about something they have done.

original environment. Time-outs should never last longer than a few minutes.

Dogs don't understand physical punishment

Dogs interpret physical punishment as a social encounter. If you punish your dog by lightly tapping his muzzle he is likely to interpret this as the initiation of a game: your 'punishment' may thus reinforce the behaviour you think you are punishing.

Above If you can get your dog to follow a treat in your hand, you will be able to teach him all he needs to know without ever having to use physical force.

If you hit your dog hard, she will see you as aggressive, assertive and as an initiator of conflict, rather than perceive your behaviour as the consequence of her own actions.

Dogs typically respond to harsh physical punishment by showing submissive or appeasing behaviour, such as cringing, hiding or even urinating. This is not an expression of guilt; it is a social response to what they perceive as an aggressive act by the person who is punishing them. A dog that behaves 'apologetically' when his owner comes home to a scene of destruction, has simply learned that he can expect aggression from the owner in that context and is doing his best to avoid it.

Dogs that are physically punished soon learn that people are violent and unpredictable. Dogs rarely make the connection between their own behaviour and the punishment that follows it.

Fear and aggression: fallout of punishment

Harsh physical punishment that causes pain and/or fear can lead to dogs showing aggression towards people, and a fear of people or situations, as well as extreme shyness and submissive urination. Dogs that are repeatedly punished will eventually learn to fear people, and may try to defend themselves against what they perceive to be displays of aggression. They will respond with aggression themselves and may learn to do this even in contexts other than those in which punishment occurs.

Learned helplessness

Dogs exposed to abusive treatment develop learned helplessness – they learn that punishment is inevitable and that nothing they can do will change this. Such animals become passive, withdrawn, nervous and disinterested. They are usually unwilling to try out new behaviours, and often appear stubborn as a result. They do not play, may refuse food and toys, are not responsive to petting and seem to have an unusually high pain threshold. These dogs can only be rehabilitated with a great deal of patience and compassion.

How do I get a dog to do something without using force?

Use a toy or treat to lure a dog into performing certain behaviours. This is called 'luring' a behaviour. You can also capture behaviours simply by waiting for the dog to offer it voluntarily. For example, most dogs sit at some point when there is nothing else to do. This does require patience, but the impression on the dog when a huge reward directly follows his behaviour is worth the wait. Shaping (see p32) is used to achieve more complex behaviour.

Let's get started with training

How often and how long?

Aim for at least one structured training session a day. Short, frequent periods have the most impact. Three 10-minute sessions per day are better than one 30-minute sitting.

Make a commitment that you will train every day. Even three minutes is better than nothing if you really cannot spare the time. Just don't let life get in the way of a great relationship between you and your dog.

Equipment

Use a flat, lightweight collar and a lead preferably made of nylon, webbing or leather – not a chain. A head collar is a very useful training aid. It resembles a horse's halter and works by controlling the movement of the head. The

Left Head collars provide effective and humane control, especially for dogs that tend to pull a lot on the lead.
Above Use a flat collar and lead. Do not use chains or other collars that cause the dog to choke.

collar goes over the top of the dog's muzzle and behind the back of the ears. The lead attaches to a ring below the chin. Head collars do not hurt the dog. Like a neck collar, you should introduce it gradually.

You can also use a body harness. Although some designs may favour pulling, specially designed anti-pulling harnesses are available. You can use an extendable lead, but this is often difficult to use with an uncontrollable dog – you may be better off using a plain lead to teach your dog self-control and relaxation, and then revert to the extendable lead later.

How to reward good behaviour

The secret is to catch your dog doing something right and then reward her immediately. She will repeat what you reward. Establish what your dog finds rewarding – different things motivate different dogs. Try these food treats (the tastier the better, but keep them small – no bigger than a thumbnail):

- Cheese
- Chicken
- Sausages
- Savoury biscuits
- Ham
- Beef
- Processed meat
- Liver spread
- Commercial dog treats

Any of the following rewards:

- A favourite toy – some (not all) dogs are wild about balls or other toys
- A game – tug, hide-and-seek and fetch
- Petting

Above *Provide tasty, soft treats like meat and cheese.*

Environmental rewards:

• Sniffing at a lamppost

• Greeting a person

Food treats are effective and easy to use, and should form the mainstay of your reward system, especially at the beginning of the training programme.

Aim to use a variety of different treats so that your dog will not become bored with the idea and will continue to look forward to his rewards eagerly.

Environmental rewards

The environment rewards many unwanted behaviours. The dog that shreds the rubbish bag has learned that tearing it open produces edible rewards. The dog that lead-pulls has learnt that pulling forward on the lead results in it getting to those places along the pavement that it wants to investigate. The 'escape artist' learns that jumping over the fence produces a

Above The dog in front is focusing on her handler, while the other dog is unaware of his handler. The golden retriever is rewarded with treats for looking at her handler, while the German shepherd enjoys environmental rewards (smells on the ground).

world of fascinating smells, sights and social encounters.

Use environmental rewards to your advantage by making them depend on good behaviour. For example, before your dog gets to sniff the lamppost, he must walk on a loose lead for a few paces; or before he gets to chase around on the lawn outside, he must sit quietly while you open the door.

Social rewards

Dogs find just about any type of social interaction rewarding. This means that many of them are sure to like the following:

How do dogs learn the meaning of words?

Dogs do not have an inherent ability to understand the meaning of words. Just because most people use the word 'sit' when instructing their dog to sit, does not mean that dogs automatically know the literal meaning of the word 'sit'. They learn the meaning of words through the repeated association of certain sounds or phrases with certain actions. If you choose to

Above left Pushing the dog away as it jumps actually reinforces the jumping behaviour.
Below *This dog is responding to a visual cue for lying down – the handler's body leaning forward and the pointed finger..*

• Being pushed out of the way or touched
• Being addressed (even shouted at)
• Being looked at or acknowledged

Have you ever done one of these things when your dog was being a nuisance? Then you have probably unwittingly rewarded the behaviour, instead of stopping it. Any form of physical interaction, verbal communication or eye contact can be rewarding to your dog, even if you intended it as a negative interaction! (Negative attention is still attention.) Social rewards are responsible for nuisance behaviours like jumping up, pawing and mouthing. To reduce the frequency of such behaviour, you must learn not to respond with any form of social interaction (see Chapters 4 and 8).

use the word 'chop' as an instruction for your dog to sit, and 'bone' for lying down, that would be perfectly fine as long as you always used the same word for the same instruction.

Visual cues vs verbal cues

I prefer the word 'cue' to 'command'. Dogs do not only respond to verbal cues, but also to other signals. They are particularly sensitive to visual signals or cues such as a pointed finger or a hand held up with the palm facing forward. In fact, very often when we think a dog is responding to a verbal cue, it is in fact noticing the often inadvertent accompanying hand or body signal. A cue is anything that the dog interprets as a sign to perform an action. The cue for sitting could be the word 'sit', a pointed finger or both. The doorbell may be the cue for rushing to the door; thirst the cue for drinking water. Dogs often respond to very subtle cues: an owner lifting his eyebrows a millimetre could make a dog slink out of a forbidden room; fleeting eye contact could make it break its stay.

The more aware you become of the cues your dog sees and hears, the better you will understand his behaviour. Observe your dog and see what cues exist for different behaviours, even if they are not cues you have

Below *A clicker training class in progress. Although the dogs can hear other handlers clicking, they know which is 'their' click, and do not become confused by all the clicking sounds.*

consciously taught your dog to react to. Environmental cues, also known as stimuli, often trigger problem behaviour.

Clicker training

Clicker training is a training method that applies the principles of operant conditioning and positive reinforcement. The clicker is a plastic device that makes a clicking sound. The click is associated with a food treat and is used to indicate to the dog what she has done right. Clicker training is extremely effective. It produces relaxed, confident dogs keen on learning new skills and enhances positive interaction between dog and handler.

Traditional training methods focus on correcting dogs for wrong behaviour and comprise jerks on choke chains, physical manipulation and force. In these instances, the dog learns to do things in order to avoid something negative, and is often too scared to try anything new in case it will be followed by a correction. Dogs trained with force and punishment are tense and anxious and learn to be reactive in order to avoid being punished.

Space does not allow for a full review of clicker training. However, there are many excellent resources available on clicker training (see Contacts & further reading). Use them and develop a skill that will stand you in good stead. As with any skill, you will have to practise clicker training. The benefits are immense – you will develop a great channel of communication for you and your dog. Clickers can be ordered on the Internet (see Contacts & further reading) and at most pet stores.

Above Click first, then give the treat. Count one-two-three after the click, before you give the treat, so that the treat does not pre-empt the click. The clicker below is attached to a wristband to make training easier.

You don't have to use the clicker; you can use food and other rewards alone. The advantages of clicker training are that you can teach precision behaviours faster and more accurately and that your dog will be less obsessed with food as it works for the click rather than the edible reward.

This section provides a short introduction to clicker training. You can read more about specific behaviours in chapters 6 and 7.

Arm yourself with a supply of treats and your clicker. At first you may find it easier to use a food pouch on your body so that the treats are easily accessible.

Click, count to three and give your dog a treat. Click first, then treat. You must follow every click with a treat. Repeat this several times and in different places. Continue for several minutes – click and treat, click and treat. The purpose of this exercise is to get your dog used to the sound of the clicker and most importantly, to enable him to make a connection between the click and the reward – when your dog hears the click, he must know that a reward is on its way. Continue for one or several sessions, until the dog shows definite interest in the click.

Use the clicker to communicate

Once your dog understands that a click means a treat is on its way, you can use it to tell your

Above *A food lure is used to help the dog into the right position to begin the roll-over. Initially, he is clicked repeatedly at this point, until he becomes fluent in performing the full roll-over.*

Above right *The click occurs as the dog performs the jump. He gets the treat afterwards.*

dog what she has done right. It is an event marker and a reward predictor. Click the instant she behaves correctly. If you are training her to sit, click the instant she does so. If you are training her to lie down, click the instant her hindquarters and chest are both on the floor at the same time. Follow every click with a treat. The timing of the click is extremely important – it must coincide with the behaviour. Give the treat after the click. (It is the click that tells the dog what she has done right, no matter what your dog is doing when she gets the treat.)

Let the clicker do the talking

During your initial training, any talking will confuse your dog. Keep quiet and use the clicker to give him accurate feedback about his behaviour. He will learn to listen for the sound. You will start using verbal cues at a later stage.

Get the behaviour, mark and reward it

To get your dog to offer a specific behaviour, use luring, capturing or shaping. Help her along, but never force her. Your dog must always think that this was her idea. Operant conditioning (see p29) is about voluntary action – the dog must make the choice about what to do, depending on the consequence you provide for the behaviour she offers. The click gives her an immediate positive consequence, therefore she will repeat those behaviours associated with the clicks.

Even if you have to wait several minutes for your dog to offer a response, it is worth the wait. Resist the temptation to push or pull – once she realizes that her own action brought about a reward she will be keen to try again. You can click for anything that resembles the final outcome you are anticipating. For 'roll over', you can click first for your dog flopping onto one side, then for going on her back and finally for the full roll over.

The click marks the action, followed by the treat, which rewards the behaviour. This is the sequence you always follow – get the action, mark and reward it.

Work in batches

Do several consecutive repetitions of a particular action. One batch can consist of anything between 5 and 20 repetitions. Work on two or three different actions per session and separate the batches either by moving to another location or by taking a short break.

Do 10 'sits' in the kitchen and 10 'downs' in the front garden, for example. Reward only the behaviour that you are working on in a particular batch, even if your dog offers perfect versions of something else. The idea is to get the dog to

Below The first step in teaching a dog how to retrieve is teaching her to 'hold' an item without dropping it.

Above *Reward anything close to the final behaviour. Don't expect the dog to hold an object perfectly at the start of your training.*

repeat the same behaviour fluently a few times, without hesitating in between repetitions.

At first, your dog may be confused about what response to offer. Guide him by using a treat as a lure, but try not to interfere. The sooner he learns that he has the choice of offering an action, the sooner he will learn to try out different things to see which you will reinforce. It doesn't matter if he is a little confused in the beginning.

Name the behaviour

Once your dog deliberately offers a behaviour, obviously expecting a click and treat, a few times in a row, you can give the behaviour a name. This is also referred to as 'adding the cue'. The process of adding the cue is described in detail in Chapter 6.

Perfect the behaviour

Once the dog responds to the cue, make sure that you get the behaviour to the standard you want. You may want a higher paw lift, or a longer sit or a better walk-along. Perfecting a behaviour is explained in detail in Chapter 6.

Fade the click and the treat

When your dog responds consistently to a cue, gradually fade the click and the treat. Instead of clicking and treating every time she does something right, click and treat eight out of 10 times. Over time, reduce the clicking and treating further until you only click and treat once in ten times. Replace the click and treat with petting and verbal praise. Finally, work without the clicker and only use it to teach new behaviours or to reinforce existing skills once in a while.

Summary: Steps of clicker training

- Get the behaviour by luring your dog with a treat, capturing the behaviour or shaping it.
- Mark it by clicking the instant she does the right thing and then give a treat. Every click is followed by a treat. The click tells the dog that she did the right thing and will get a reward.
- Name the behaviour by associating it with a verbal or visual cue, or both, once she does it spontaneously and fluently (see page 99).
- Perfect the behaviour by rewarding better versions.
- Gradually fade both the click and treat at the same time.

Make it easy for your dog to succeed

Set small realistic goals when teaching your dog a new skill. Initially, make things really easy and reward even the tiniest inkling of good behaviour. As your dog starts to volunteer more good behaviour, increase your standards. At first, he may only sit for a few seconds when greeting people. Make it worth his while by rewarding short sits generously. As he gets better, increase the duration before rewarding it. Always surprise him with an unexpectedly easy reward now and then, even as the training becomes more and more sophisticated. Unexpected rewards will keep your dog on his toes.

Why do dogs forget what they learn?

Anybody who has ever trained a dog will experience it at some time: a dog that is capable of performing a particular skill will appear to have forgotten all that he has learned. You know how well your dog can do this particular trick, and you

Although this dog can perform a good sit-stay with no distractions (top), the handler expects less (shorter distance and duration) when introducing new distractions (above).

have told everybody about it, but he is just not performing when you have an audience. This may be embarrassing, but it is not uncommon.

The context has changed

Dogs are very context-bound: they learn to do something in a specific environment, under specific conditions. To them that is part of the learning. A dog may do a perfect 'sit-stay' at home in the kitchen with you wearing your slippers, but when he is in the park the context is different and he has to learn that 'sit-stays'

are the same in the park as in the kitchen. New contexts also usually mean new distractions.

You may need to teach an existing skill again in the presence of a new distraction. Every time you retrain your dog in a new context or with a new distraction, it will become easier and he will learn progressively faster each time.

Reduced motivation

Your dog may not be motivated sufficiently to perform according to the set standard. A more difficult context, such as a new place with many distractions, requires a higher quality reward. Try the following to increase your dog's motivation:

- Use exceptionally tasty treats – a high-quality reward
- Use a variety of treats – an unpredictable reward
- Train when she is likely to be hungry – shortly before feeding time
- Use friendly and encouraging body language (see Chapter 5) – if you are in a bad mood this will rub off on your dog
- Use her favourite toy only when you need to motivate her
- Build up a favourable history of reinforcement – many rewards for good behaviour
- Use rewards generously and frequently
- Ensure that your timing is correct and that you are consistent – if you confuse your dog she will become less motivated

Left This young German shepherd puppy is learning from an early age that walking with a slack lead really works.

What is the best age to train a dog?

The younger your dog is when you start training, the better. If a dog can learn all the right habits early on, it is very unlikely that he will develop bad habits. You can train puppies from as young as two months of age (and even younger). Those between two and four months of age are extremely receptive to training due to their inherent receptiveness to environmental stimuli at this age.

If you use the principles of operant conditioning and positive reinforcement to train your dog, it is not necessary to wait until he is six months or older before commencing training. By six months, a puppy has already had ample opportunity to learn all the wrong things. It is easier to work with a 'clean slate' than to have to address existing inappropriate learning.

Can you train old dogs?

Yes, you can indeed teach old dogs new tricks! Though it is easier with a young, unspoiled puppy, it is never too late to start training a dog. The use of ample rewards and patience will pay off with even the most resistant old dog. Some dogs have become so hardened by previous inappropriate training methods that they are hesitant and unwilling at first, but once they trust the person training them, they do come around.

Right Even older dogs benefit from the mental stimulation of regular training sessions.

Chapter 3

The learning environment

LEARNING IS EASIER AND MORE EFFECTIVE IN AN environment that is conducive to successful training. This includes the immediate physical environment where formal training sessions take place, as well as the environment outside this structured context where your dog has his daily experiences and interactions and where informal learning takes place. Both the physical environment and the dog's mental and physical health are important in facilitating this process. Possibly the most important factor affecting how well your dog learns is the role you play in his life. Social relationships have a marked effect on his ability to learn and on his general behaviour. This chapter deals with creating the best physical environment for your dog's structured and informal learning, while the following addresses his or her social needs.

The ideal environment

Always start training in a place with minimal distractions. It should be familiar to your dog, but not contain too much of interest, as she should not find the environment more interesting than you. The most common distractions are people, other dogs, unfamiliar sights, sounds and smells and moving objects.

Work in many different locations

Once your dog can perform to a satisfactory level in a known environment, move to other locations, also with minimal distractions. Go to the kitchen, bedroom and back garden, but only start adding distractions once your dog has associated training with a few different locations. Every time you move to a new place, your dog will think everything has changed, including everything he has already learnt. You will have to re-train him every time there is a new location or distraction. Your dog will find it progressively easier, however, to adjust to changes the more you expose him to variety.

Introduce distractions gradually

When you start working with distractions, make sure that at first they are not overwhelming. For instance, work with other dogs at a considerable distance at first or play the radio very softly. Gradually increase the intensity of the distractions as he learns to cope better.

> *Generalization refers to the ability to apply what is learned in one environment to a different environment*

Opposite *Start training in an environment that is familiar to your dog and has few or no distractions.*

Reward more for less at difficult times

When you change the training environment, anticipate that it will be more difficult for your dog to perform, and ensure you have extra tasty treats with you as rewards. Make it easy to earn rewards in challenging circumstances – give bigger rewards more frequently than you would otherwise.

Be patient

If you attend dog-training classes, do not expect your dog to learn much the first few sessions. Usually the presence of other dogs and people, coupled with the new place, is so exciting that it overrides everything else. If you can only do five minutes of productive training during the hour, then consider that already a good start. Always work a little distance away from the other handlers and dogs at first; this will make it easier for your dog to focus on you.

Make sure your dog is fit and healthy

Ensure your dog is physically healthy. Pain and discomfort not only result in a lack of motivation, but can also cause anxiety and unexpected aggression. If your previously highly motivated dog is suddenly listless and disinterested, have a vet check her out before you expect her to do any more work.

Although this dog knows how to weave through the poles (above), she needs more valuable rewards more frequently when expected to perform in the presence of another dog (left).

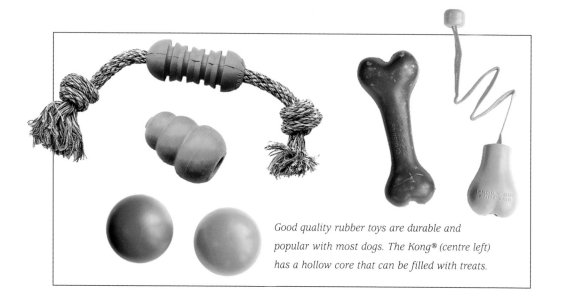

Good quality rubber toys are durable and popular with most dogs. The Kong® (centre left) has a hollow core that can be filled with treats.

Keep training sessions short and sweet

Training should always be fun for you and your dog. Short and frequent sessions are better than long and rare ones. Always end training before your dog loses interest, no matter how short the session is. Some dogs, can, at first, only concentrate for three or four minutes. With time, they will be eager to engage in longer sessions.

The ideal environment for informal learning

Even if you are a super-person and can afford to spend a full hour every day training your dog and allow for 10 hours of sleep per dog per day, formal learning will still only account for 7% of your dog's waking time. What happens to your dog during the remaining 93% of the time can have a profound effect on how he performs during formal training, and his general behaviour.

An enriched environment

Provide your dog with an interesting environment full of adequate mental and physical stimulation, particularly at times when he is on his own.

Let your dog have a choice of toys to play with, activities to engage in and places where he can enjoy these activities. The more choice you can provide, the better. You can even go so far as to provide a variety of surfaces, such as grass, soil, flooring and paving, as well as different stimuli, such as a radio, music and scents.

However, don't make it easy for your dog to misbehave! Keep chewable objects that are not intended for canine entertainment out of reach and ensure that the area your dog is left in is properly enclosed to prevent escape. You can offer attractive opportunities for good behaviour by providing an enriched, canine-friendly environment.

Breed-specific needs

Find out more about the breed of your dog. The type of dog may be obvious from his appearance; if it is a mixed breed, you may know the breed of the mother. Find out the original function of the breed and how this could affect your dog's behaviour and needs, and enable you to meet them more effectively.

Herding dogs and terriers are very active and need to be given constructive activities to keep them physically and mentally occupied. They are high-maintenance breeds, and owners need to spend lots of time to ensure they are adequately stimulated, both mentally and physically. When herding dogs such as Border collies are used on farms, they work most days for the whole day. If that is what they were bred to do, it makes sense that they be constantly active. Gundogs such as retrievers, pointers and setters are also working dogs and enjoy carrying things around in their mouths. Retrievers particularly enjoy water and swimming. Terriers and dachshunds, on the other hand, were bred to find prey underground, hence they enjoy digging and playing with 'prey-like' toys – for example, squeaky and bouncy toys.

Find creative ways of channelling your dog's energy into activities that he or she will enjoy. Dogs that do not have high levels of physical activity, such as Bassets and St Bernards, for example, still need mental stimulation and regular social interaction.

Below Sheep-herding breeds like the bearded collie and Australian shepherd have high activity levels and need a lot of exercise.

Suggested dog breeds for different types of accommodation

Small urban accommodation	Large urban accommodation	Farm
Basset	Afghan Hound	Anatolian Shepherd
Bichon Frise	Airedale Terrier	Australian Cattle Dog
Bloodhound	Alaskan Malamute	Border Collie
Bullmastiff	Beagle	English foxhound
Cavalier King Charles Spaniel	Bouvier	Greyhound
Chow Chow	Boxer	Irish Wolfhound
Corgi	Dachshund	Jack Russell terrier
English Bulldog	Dalmatian	Parson Jack Russell terrier
French Bulldog	Doberman	Siberian Husky
Italian Greyhound	German Shepherd	
Maltese	Golden retriever	
Norfolk terrier	Labrador retriever	
Norwich terrier	Saluki	
Pekingese	Schnauzers	
Pomeranian	Staffordshire bull terrier	
Pug	Rhodesian Ridgeback	
Whippet	Rough Collie	
Yorkshire Terrier	Smooth Collie	
	Weimaraner	

Do big dogs need more space?

No, but it depends on the breed. Jack Russell terriers and dachshunds, for example, are small but active breeds that require a lot of space and have a tendency to bark a lot. They are not well suited to a small property. Bullmastiffs and Chow Chows are large breeds with medium to low activity levels that require less space in proportion to their size. Refer to the table above for examples of breeds likely to fit into a specific environment. These are broad guidelines only, as any dog's ultimate behaviour does not depend only on its genetic (breed) background, but also on how it is socialized and trained.

What breeds are good watchdogs?

People often have a need for a good watchdog. The function of a watchdog is to alert the owner by barking. A watchdog should not bark excessively – only when there is a good reason for it. A watchdog need not be aggressive.

Examples of good watchdogs are:
- Chihuahua
- German Shepherd
- Lhasa Apso
- Pomeranians
- Rhodesian Ridgeback
- Rottweilers
- Schnauzers
- Terriers (all)

Occupy the jaws

Dogs use their muzzles in much the same way humans use their hands when playing or eating. Dogs are, after all, predators and therefore their jaws were designed to grab, shake and chew.

Provide your dog with a variety of chew toys, so that it does not chew on inappropriate things like irrigation pipes or table legs (or human limbs, as is common with puppies). Make the toys more attractive by smearing tasty spreads on them or stuffing them with food, and vary them by including 'consumables' like rawhides and cow hooves, and 'non-consumables' like strong rubber toys. Bones are good if, and only if, they are large marrow-bones, otherwise they can cause intestinal obstructions when swallowed.

Food-dispensing toys are excellent as they provide mental stimulation (dogs develop problem-solving skills since they have to figure out how to get the food out of the toy) and physical stimulation in the form of chasing. The best food-dispensing toys are the adjustable ones that allow you to change the amount of food they let through. (You can increase the level of difficulty as your dog becomes more adept at solving the food puzzle.) Toys that can be stuffed with food provide hours of activity for food-motivated dogs.

The Kong® is an old favourite, providing some interactive play through its unpredictable

***Left** The German Shepherd makes an excellent watchdog, but has a tendency to bark excessively.*

bounce. Many variations of this original are available. You can also fill a hollow toy with a liquid and freeze it to provide a stimulating yet refreshing toy on a hot day.

Balls and rings are great fun for dogs and humans alike. They come in myriad sizes, styles and textures – try out different ones and see what works for your dog. Tug toys also come in many shapes and sizes. Play tug games only if you can control access to the toy. If your dog is stronger than you and always 'wins', first spend some time teaching it to release toys (see Chapter 7) before you continue playing tug games. (More about games in Chapter 4). Squeaky toys can be great fun, but can cause excessive arousal in some dogs. If your dog is highly obsessed with a squeaky toy, tearing out the 'squeak' and not wanting to relinquish it,

Above The Buster Cube® is an excellent food-dispensing toy. Show your dog how to use it at first by rolling it around for him so that he can see where the food comes out.

then avoid these toys and stick to games that enhance self-control.

Other toy ideas include frozen cloths (wet a kitchen cloth, wring and knot it, and place it in the freezer), ice cubes, real bones filled with peanut butter and large plastic bottles with a hole and some food pellets inside (not suitable for highly destructive dogs as they may ingest bits of plastic).

Not all dogs are toy-crazy, and some have a very specific taste in toys. Try different types until you find those your dog prefers.

Choice of activities and olfactory stimulation

Provide a choice of activities for your dog while she is alone. Apart from food-dispensing and interactive (bouncy) toys, you can set up a treasure hunt by leaving a trail of dog pellets that she can discover after you have left. You can also hide interesting, smelly things (food or cow dung) in various places she has access to, thereby stimulating her sense of smell. Bury something with a strong scent in a garden patch that you don't mind having dug up. Hang toys from trees or beams.

Activities you can participate in together include walks, training, games and organized dog sport like obedience classes, agility, tracking, lure coursing and many more. Once your dog is well trained you could even consider joining a therapy team.

Choice of locations

The more locations your dog has access to, the more interesting it will find the environment. Ensure he has more than one resting place – one in the sun and another in the shade; one sheltered, one in the open; one enclosed, one with a view. You can provide these options both indoors and out, depending on where your dog spends most of his time and your home environment.

Provide visual stimulation by giving your dog access to a lookout point – something high, but safe, from where he can see out. This could comprise an elaborate do-it-yourself canine jungle gym or simply access to a balcony or windowsill. For the outdoors dog, uneven or terraced gardens are ideal as they provide

***Above** Leave a food trail for your dog to keep her busy when she is alone. Remember to reduce her daily food ration by the amount of food you use for treasure hunts and food-dispensing toys.*

different levels and thus more choices. Hiding and resting places underneath shrubs and in depressions provide even more mental stimulation for the canine brain.

Physical exercise

There is a common perception that a lack of physical exercise is the main reason for canine behavioural problems. While there certainly is some truth in such a statement, it should be qualified: dogs that were bred to be physically active, like herding dogs and terriers, certainly need a lot of physical exercise. However, there is a danger that by encouraging uninhibited exercise, dogs may become less capable of self-control and this could contribute to other problems. By all means, encourage your dog to exercise as much as possible, but maintain control by calling him back to you at regular intervals and interspersing the physical activity with self-control exercises (see Chapter 6).

Another way of encouraging self-control in your dog is to teach him to sit quietly so that you can attach his lead. Ask him to sit and attach the lead only if he sits. As soon as he gets excited, remove the lead, put it down and continue doing something else, ignoring the dog. As soon as he calms down, proceed again with attaching the lead. This teaches the dog that the lead comes on (and the walk happens) only if he can demonstrate calm and controlled behaviour.

Many dogs were not bred for high levels of physical activity. Bulldogs and Bassets, for example, are not exactly the epitome of streamlined athleticism and do not have the capacity for heavy exercise. Breeds with flat faces (brachycephalic breeds) have difficulty breathing and dissipating body heat. As a result, they are prone to hyperthermia (over-heating). You should not exercise brachycephalic dogs in the heat of the day, or excessively at any time. You should also not confine them to small spaces with poor ventilation such as

a closed car. Symptoms of hyperthermia include panting, a high body temperature and collapse. In such cases, immediately immersing the dog in cool water and giving him access to cool air is required.

You should provide your dog with opportunities for exercise on a regular basis. If he has a high activity level, this should be at least once a day. You can provide the average dog with good exercise through regular walks, swimming and ball games. Irregular exercise promotes over-excitement and uncontrollability. Stick to a routine time even if it is not exactly the same every day.

> *Provide controlled,*
> *regular exercise*

Above *Teach your dog to sit quietly when you are putting his the collar and lead on him.*

Mental stimulation

Lack of mental stimulation is possibly as common a cause of behaviour problems in dogs as a lack of physical exercise – if not more so. Mental stimulation can be offered by providing a variety of activities and toys as described above, structured training and access to visual and olfactory stimuli. Aim for at least one training session daily, even if it is only five minutes long. Three or more short sessions per day are the ideal. Training sessions need not exceed 20 minutes and should be enjoyable for your dog. Take a break every few minutes during the course of a session, playing a game or giving a tummy tickle.

A walk a day keeps the madness away

Above *Allow your dog to sniff and investigate on walks, particularly if she seems nervous about a specific object or smell. Let her get used to it in her own time.*

Not only does a daily walk provide your dog with physical exercise, it also stimulates her mind, as there are interesting things to see and smell. Allow your dog to sniff and investigate every now and then, but don't let her control the walk completely. Let her sniff and have fun as a reward for walking nicely on a slack lead focusing on you.

Habituation

Habituation refers to getting a dog used to new stimuli in the environment. It specifically refers to inanimate stimuli; in other words, things and experiences, as opposed to live creatures. The best time to habituate a dog is during the sensitive period of early puppyhood, between two and four months. Expose a puppy to car rides, household appliances and their sounds, being examined on a table, things with wheels, plastic bags and umbrellas. These experiences should always be pleasant.

You can also habituate an older dog to new stimuli by exposure to a pleasant and controlled environment. A negative or traumatic experience can have the opposite effect and can result in a fear or phobia of a certain situation or object. Systematic desensitization and counter-conditioning (see Chapter 9) are required to deal with existing fears and phobias.

Socialization

The process of getting used to people, other dogs and other animals is called socialization.

Again, the young puppy is far more receptive to accepting social contact. Older dogs can learn to socialize, but it takes a lot longer and requires considerable patience and skill. Encourage pleasant interactions between your dog and all kinds of people and other dogs, and reward her for behaving calmly. (Refer to Chapter 6 for ways of teaching your dog social skills.)

Below left *Make new experiences, such as getting into the car, pleasant for your dog right from the start.*

Below right *This German Shepherd puppy is discovering a swimming pool for the first time. He is confident and shows interest – an appropriate reaction to a new stimulus.*

Chapter 4

Social and rule structures

I N ORDER TO FEEL SAFE AND SECURE, A DOG NEEDS to trust the people he interacts with on a daily basis. This trust is created if the dog perceives the people in his social system, individually and collectively, as effective managers and trustworthy leaders. Competent managers know how to control resources effectively, and in particular understand how to manage social interactions. Good leaders provide accurate and consistent feedback about appropriate behaviour in different contexts, and set clear boundaries. With a healthy social structure and a clear rule structure, the dog knows what to expect and what is expected of him.

Resource management

Dogs become anxious if people do not manage their resources effectively. It is just like a business: as long as management is perceived to be in control, the salary earner is content. Provided the salary is received in a predictable way, there is no anxiety. However, if management is not effective, for whatever reason, the salary earner becomes anxious: he feels threatened, as his salary may be in jeopardy. In a sense, your dog is like a salary earner – she wants to be employed by you (rather than be self-employed), as she does not have the ability to effectively control resources (be a manager) herself. Dogs are happy to 'work' for their 'salary', that is, to earn their access to valuable resources. When they do not perceive the people in their lives as efficient providers, they become anxious and this anxiety is manifested in a variety of symptoms, such as excessive attention-seeking behaviour and aggression (see control-related aggression in Chapter 9).

To effectively manage our dogs' resources and help them relax, we need to understand what a dog's resources are. Resources are things that have a significant value for the dog. The most important resources for dogs are social resources and physical resources. Social resources include the following:

- Physical interaction (stroking and touching)
- Verbal communication (chatting to the dog and giving commands)
- Eye contact
- Training
- Games
- Walks
- Grooming
- Greetings

Physical resources include the following:
- Food
- Personal space

Opposite This puppy is relaxed in the presence of a visitor because he has been given clear feedback about boundaries.

Above *Stroking is a form of social interaction.*

- Territory
- Resting place
- Toys

Effective resource management is about creating consistency and predictability about privileges and rules. The trick is to show your dog that you are the main source of good things (resources). He must also understand that to obtain anything of value, he has to defer to you (listen to instructions, i.e. earn a salary). These are necessary conditions before you can expect to be successful in training. If he does not recognise you as the manager and mentor, it will be difficult to motivate him to perform for you.

A healthy social structure

In a healthy social system, the dog recognises the people in her life as the providers of privileges and the controllers of resources. The competent resource manager ensures that the dog is comfortable in the household, does not feel threatened and respects the people that make up the management system (i.e. the whole family). In a healthy social system, social interaction is mostly initiated by people, dogs do not show excessive attention-seeking behaviour, are generally relaxed and confident and are responsive to instructions from people.

Symptoms of a sick social structure

Lack of leadership and poor resource management by people causes uncertainty in dogs. If they don't get clear indications of social and rule structure, they become insecure and anxious. This anxiety contributes to a variety of behaviour problems. Symptoms of a social system that is not fulfilling a dog's needs could include the following:

- The dog initiates and controls most of the social interaction with people.
- The dog gets attention on demand all the time.
- High levels of attention-seeking behaviour (jumping, pawing, mouthing, mounting, grabbing objects, barking, nipping).
- The dog controls physical resources like toys, space on furniture, access to rooms.
- The dog ignores instructions.
- The dog is aggressive towards household members.
- Other behaviour problems like compulsive behaviour, interdog aggression and house-

soiling (there can also be other reasons for these behaviours).

Manage social interactions: Interact on your terms

Your interactions with your dog should be structured and controlled. Social interaction should occur regularly and be pleasant for the dog.

To be in control of social interaction, you should be the one who initiates and ends the majority of such interactions (see the list on p66). If your dog can successfully elicit a reaction from you every time he or she wants your attention, then you are not controlling the interaction.

You should initiate and control these interactions most of the time, not the dog. You shouldn't scratch the dog behind his ears because he shoved his muzzle under your arm. You shouldn't talk to the dog because he sat there whining. You should caress, talk to, touch and play with your dog because you have decided it is the right time to do so. The right time is when the dog is calm and relaxed and not insisting on attention.

Your dog will quickly learn that quiet and calm behaviour results in interaction and will become less demanding. Don't give attention when he demands or expects it, but rather anticipate your dog's needs and initiate interaction before he insists on it. If he has already initiated an interaction, learn not to respond to it. This is the difficult part – ignoring your dog when he is asking for attention.

When a dog asks for attention, he is not necessarily looking for affection. In many cases, he is asking for feedback about who is in

Top *Ensure that your dog perceives grooming as a positive social interaction by introducing it gradually and at an early age.*

Above *Regular play is an important social interaction. Ensure that the game takes place on your terms.*

control. If you simply comply and react all the time, you are saying to him that he controls social interaction – whenever he wants it, he gets it. This makes him anxious as he is not equipped to be the resource manager, he needs you to handle that.

How do I know that my dog is initiating interaction?

Dogs use various methods to initiate social interaction, including what could be termed as 'normal' attention-getting behaviours, for example:

- Pawing
- Jumping
- Staring (eyeing)
- Barking or whining

Some dogs can develop more invasive, and even creative, ways of getting attention, such as the following:

- Mouthing (arms, hands)
- Mounting (legs)
- Grabbing objects and running away to initiate a chase game
- Bringing the ball and putting it down at your feet to initiate a fetch game
- Nipping at feet, arms, clothes – this always gets a reaction!
- Licking
- Barking or whining
- Chewing on forbidden objects in your presence
- Messing inside the house

Most of these attention-seeking behaviours can be perfectly normal if they occur infrequently, but when they are excessive they become part of a vicious cycle. The more attention the dog gets in response to attention-seeking behaviour, the more he craves attention and the attention-seeking behaviour simply intensifies.

Ignore does not mean doing nothing

If your dog does nag you for attention, learn to actively ignore him. Don't just do nothing – do the following (also known as 'offering the cold shoulder'):

- Look the other way (a mere glance can reinforce the attention-seeking behaviour).
- Keep your hands to yourself – folding your arms is quite effective.
- Keep quiet – this is often the most difficult part!

Above *The dog's jumping is reinforced by physical contact, eye contact and verbal communication.*

- Turn your back (if you're standing), or your shoulders (if you're sitting), so that the dog sees your back.
- Walk away if necessary.
- If your dog is highly aroused, it may be necessary to isolate her for a few minutes until she calms down.

Use your body language to indicate to the dog that you are not interacting at this time and wait for him to calm down and stop performing the attention-seeking behaviour. As soon as he stops and relaxes, you can give him attention (controlled attention – you don't want to excite the dog all over again). This way he learns that being calm and controlled yields positive results.

Rowdy homecomings

Excessive excitement by dogs upon their owner's arrival at home is common and a very good example of how our own behaviour can have a marked impact on our dogs' behaviour. The way people behave in this situation usually reinforces hyper-excitement at homecoming. Owners tend to get just as excited greeting their dogs as the dogs do greeting them. This teaches the dogs that it is acceptable to get excited at greeting times.

Instead, when arriving home you should offer the 'cold shoulder', as described above; wait for the dog to calm down and then initiate a controlled interaction. The dog will learn very quickly that the sooner she calms down, the sooner she will get any interaction. The secret is to completely ignore her, until she relaxes. At first it may take a while before

Above *When the dog is offered the cold shoulder, she stops jumping and calms down.*

she does calm down, but after a few days of offering the cold shoulder at homecomings, she will be much calmer and more controlled. Arriving home should always be a civilized affair.

Emotional departures

Some dogs become quite distressed when their owners leave the home. They hyperventilate, shiver, vocalize and even physically try to prevent the person from leaving.

This could simply be a conditioned response or an indication of a serious underlying anxiety (see Chapter 9). If departure distress is a conditioned response, it can be unlearned. Find out what makes the dog anxious – is it picking up the keys or putting on a coat? Then desensitize the dog to these departure cues by going through the departure routine several times – when you are not planning on leaving. Give your dog a chew or other toy to occupy him, and ignore him for half an hour before (and while) leaving. Don't say goodbye (he won't be offended). The more you reassure an already anxious dog, the worse the anxiety will become. The less fuss you make of coming and going, the easier it will be for your dog.

Plan your interactions

Fulfilling your dog's social needs requires that you plan and anticipate how you will interact with her. It requires a change from being reactive (waiting for the dog to do something and reacting to it) to being proactive (anticipating when and how interaction is required and providing it at the right time).

Dogs do not need or want constant attention. Your dog will be happy to wait for her quality time if she knows that there will be such time at regular intervals. Provide regular, positive interaction and be consistent and predictable. Ensure that you initiate (and conclude on your terms) at least two activities per day. These activities could include any of the following:

• A training session
• Playing a game
• Going for a walk or run
• Grooming
• Massaging
• Stroking and talking

Left Stroke your dog as long as she is calm and controlled, and not because she insists on it.

Whatever the activity you engage in, keep in mind the following criteria:

- It must be something you and your dog enjoy.
- You must be the one to initiate the interaction.
- You must be the one to conclude the interaction.
- Don't do it when the dog is misbehaving. Ignore misbehaviour as described above, and try again as soon as she has calmed down.

It doesn't really matter for how long the interaction continues – anything from five or ten minutes will be adequate. The longer the better, but more frequent, shorter interactions are better than just one long session.

Above: *Plan regular quality time with your dog. Agility training provides both exercise and an opportunity for good social interaction.*

Be predictable

For a dog, a predictable environment is a safe environment. A normal, healthy dog needs routines that are maintained fairly uniformly. Some dogs can develop resource-control related aggression, in which case you need to make their routines slightly less predictable. (Read more about it in Chapter 9.)

All dogs need clear and predictable feedback about their actions. Don't allow something sometimes and not at other times. If you are consistent, your dog will learn faster.

Above: Hug and cuddle your dog if he enjoys it – but don't overdo it.

Can I still love my dog?

Yes, of course! You can still cuddle your dog and talk sweetly to him (if that is what you like doing), but do it on your terms. Respect your dog's needs – most dogs do not like people in their faces all day long. They often put up with it because they have no other choice. Make sure that your relationship with your dog is based on what is good for your dog, and not only on your own personal needs.

Games

Playing games is a wonderful way of interacting with your dog. You can play fetch, hide-and-seek and tug games. As with any game, there are rules, the most important one being that you should not allow the games to get out of control.

It is better if you play with your dog with a toy of some sort. Do not let your dog get used to grabbing your arms and legs in jest. This can easily result in unnecessary injury if the dog gets overexcited. As much fun as they are for so many people, rough wrestling games with dogs can be potentially dangerous, as they can so readily get out of hand and because a dog's jaws are capable of causing serious damage. Dogs use their jaws as we use our hands – so whenever they become aroused they are likely to use them. Although injuries during playtime are usually unintended, play can quite suddenly escalate into aggression.

Stop the game when it gets rough – just freeze, get up and leave. Next time, stop before it gets to this stage and redirect the dog to an appropriate toy. Remember that you must be the one to initiate and terminate the game.

Tug games are great fun for dogs, but only play them if you can control access to the toy. You can tug and let the dog 'win' a few times, but ultimately you must be able to take control of the toy and put it away. It is best that you keep a tug toy out of reach of your dog. Only present it when you are ready to play and then take it back again afterwards. The dog can have access to another tug toy if he enjoys playing with it on his own, or with other dogs; just keep the one

Above: Control the toy during tug games – teach your dog to release it readily.

Avoid rough-and-tumble games

you will be playing with away from your dog until you are ready to play.

Dogs should be willing to relinquish objects when you instruct them to do so. Teach your dog to 'drop' or 'give' a toy or other item – refer to Chapter 6.

Walks

Dogs love walks, but this should be something that you enjoy too. Too often, it is dogs that take their owners for a walk – the dog forges ahead, with the poor person attached to the other end of the lead dragged along in quite an undignified fashion.

In order to make a walk something both you and your dog can enjoy, and something you can control, your dog needs to be aware of you throughout the walk. Some dogs do this naturally, but most dogs need to be trained to focus on their handler.

The walk belongs to you and you are entitled to control it. You can realistically expect your dog to walk next to you without pulling ahead, but when off the lead she should readily come to you when called. (See Chapter 6 for tips on building focus, and using this for heelwork and recalls.) If you control the walk, your dog will be less reactive when meeting strange people and dogs along the way, and will more likely look to you for guidance in situations with which she is unfamiliar. You and your dog will benefit from walks that you control.

Children and dogs

Ideally, dogs should be able to interact comfortably with children and should perceive the children in a household as part of the resource-management structure. This can be achieved by involving children in the daily management of the dog, for example, the child can feed the dog (under supervision) at mealtimes and feed dog treats during training sessions while the adult does the training.

Although most dogs, with the correct training and socialization from a young age, should be fine around children, certain breeds tend to fit better into a busy family life. Very sensitive dogs that have not had pleasant exposure to children in the first few months of their lives may not adapt well to family life.

The ideal children's dog is a medium-sized, confident, people-loving dog that enjoys playing and is not easily aroused to aggression. Large-breed dogs may be of even temperament, but can easily knock small children over during play. This often becomes a vicious cycle

Left This dog is exercising self-control when meeting a stranger during the course of a walk.

when the child starts screaming and running, making the dog even more excited, leading to nipping and biting.

Puppies should be taught from the start not to jump up on people or children. Children should learn how to react to boisterous dogs, to be gentle with dogs and when to leave a dog alone. This can be difficult, especially for small children and toddlers. Toddlers tend to poke, pinch and pull and are not capable of controlling their fine motor movements properly. Hence, dogs could easily perceive their actions as threatening.

All interaction between children (even up to teenager stage) and dogs should be supervised by adults. Never leave a small child and a dog alone together. Ensure that there is a safe and comfortable place where the dog can be confined when you are not there to supervise.

The very small dog breeds are not suitable for young, active children because they have very thin bones that break easily when they are dropped accidentally.

It is not only the family with small children that should consider their choice of breed carefully, but also elderly people and those with disabilities. Here, a sociable dog that is easy to train, with low excitement levels and a low need for physical exercise would be required, such as a poodle or spaniel.

Top *Teach your child to offer the cold shoulder to a boisterous dog.*
Left *The child rewards the dog for being calm and not jumping, thus giving the dog a clear and consistent message about rules.*

Breeds suitable for families with young children

Small and medium breeds

•Basenji •Beagle •Bichon Frise •Boston Terrier •Bull Terrier •Cairn Terrier •Cavalier King Charles Spaniel •Italian Greyhound •King Charles Spaniel •Lhasa Apso •Maltese •Norfolk Terrier •Norwich Terrier •Papillon •Pekingese •Pug •Shetland Sheepdog •Shih Tsu •Springer Spaniel •Staffordshire Bull Terrier •Toy Poodle •Whippet

Large breeds

•Afghan Hound •Borzoi •Boxer •Collies •Dalmatian •Great Dane •Irish Wolfhound •Newfoundland •Pointers •Retrievers •Saluki •Samoyed •Setters •Standard Poodle •Weimaraner

NOT ideal

•Akita •Anatolian Shepherd •Chow Chow

Managing physical resources

Managing the food resource – eating arrangements

When it comes to eating arrangements, you should feed your dog specific meals, as opposed to having food available all the time. It is for you – not the dog – to decide when mealtimes should be. Don't feed your dog only when he begs for food. Always expect the dog to work for his food (and his treats!), by sitting and waiting for your instructions before you feed him.

Be consistent: if the dog does not comply with your instruction, you should withhold food and try again later, or at the next feeding time. Give your instruction (only ask once), wait a few seconds and if he doesn't respond, put away the food bowl until later. He will learn very quickly that you are serious about what you want before he gets what he wants.

> *Your dog should work to earn every meal*

Leave the food out for a specified period of time, and then pick it up if it is uneaten. Generally, 10 to 15 minutes is enough time for a dog to finish his meal (many dogs eat a lot faster than this). If he is a very fussy eater, make the food more attractive by adding tasty gravy or mixing in some meat, but don't leave food out for more than 15 minutes. Do not fuss over or hand-feed the dog. Unceremoniously pick up the bowl after the allotted time and only feed again at the next feeding time. The dog will not starve – at some point he will understand what you mean and start eating immediately when you feed him. This could take a few days, but be persistent and you will have good results.

Controlled meals have several practical advantages in addition to the behavioural aspects. Food is less likely to be soiled by ants, household poisons and birds (if you feed dogs outside). You will also recognize signs of illness much sooner if your dog eats regular meals, as a drop in appetite will be much more obvious.

Personal-space management

Your dog should be willing to share her personal space. Obviously your demands should be within reason – it wouldn't be fair to constantly intrude on your dog's personal space, or do it in a way that causes distress or discomfort (as is often the case with young children), and expect her to happily accept that. However, she should allow you to touch her all over her body. Ideally, she should keep still and remain relaxed while you examine head, ears, muzzle, mouth, paws and flanks, and lift her tail.

In order to achieve this, a puppy should be handled a lot, by different people. This should always be a pleasant experience for her, associated with food and other rewards.

Be careful if your dog has a history of resisting handling, and especially of aggression when being handled. If your dog flinches, wriggles, tries to get away or growls or snaps when you handle him, it will require a gradual, systematic approach to desensitize him to handling (see Chapter 6).

Above *Examine your dog's teeth, ears and paws regularly so that he is used to being handled. Encourage him to allow others to do the same.*

Above Your dog may define her own sleeping area without having a bed there. If this is in a doorway, teach her to get up for you to pass.

Sleeping arrangements

Does your dog consider her bed or kennel her property and won't allow you to touch her when she is inside her 'den'? Prevent this by getting the puppy used to people taking over her bed, and reward her for positive, relaxed interaction with people while she is in her bed.

Climb inside your puppy's bed every so often, and move it around, just to remind her that she is really just 'renting' from you.

Do some training sessions with your dog in her bed so that she becomes used to following your instructions in and around her bed – have her sit and wait or do tricks, for rewards, in her bed. If she is aggressive when you approach, temporarily remove the bed while you work on getting the basics of resource control in place.

If your dog considers your bed her domain and won't allow your partner near it, you need to act urgently. Refer to Chapter 9 for advice on control-related aggression, but get a qualified animal behaviourist to assist you immediately. In the meantime, banish your dog from the bedroom.

Should dogs be allowed on people's beds? This is a personal choice – if you like having dogs on your furniture, go ahead and allow it. However, ideally your dog should only jump onto furniture on your invitation, and not because that is her preference or choice. Teach your dog to jump onto things in response to a cue that you only issue when you want him to jump. Free access to furniture does have its risks. People with babies find it difficult to deal with dogs that are constantly jumping onto furniture. Dogs with control-related aggression (see Chapter 9) frequently bite when ordered or made to get off furniture.

> *You decide which toys your dog has and when*

Toy control

Control toys by keeping them in a toy chest and handing them out on a rotational basis, so that your dog only has two or three toys available at any given time. Make quite a scene of picking up toys, inspecting them and handing them out again. This maintains your dog's interest in the toys and shows her that you are managing the resource effectively.

Territory management

Teach your dog how to behave at territory boundaries. She must know how to greet people at the front door, the garden gate or the outside fence (see Chapter 6). Control the areas that she has access to. She does not have to be with you all the time. Close doors between you and your dog from time to time, without any fuss. It should be a normal occurrence for your dog that at certain times she is not in your company and has to fend for herself.

Dogs that have uncontrolled access to their owners can develop separation distress because they never learn to be on their own. Teaching a puppy early on the skills to stay home alone can help alleviate this problem.

Different parts of a dog's territory have different values for the dog. The areas where people spend a lot of time, particularly where they interact with her such as the living room or kitchen, will have high value for the dog. Being aware of the relative value of a territory is useful when dealing with interdog relationships

Right Rotate toys so that your dog can see that you control them.

because dogs are more likely to fight in areas of high value. You can identify areas of high value by observing where your dog chooses or demands to spend more time.

Establishing a clear rule structure

Teach your dog the right things to do so that he will be less likely to do the wrong things. This is probably the biggest benefit of training a few basic exercises – you are giving your dog options for those times when he may be uncertain about what to do. If sitting and waiting has been reinforced countless times in the past, or doing a roll over, these are the things he will think of doing, rather than biting, barking or escaping, when he finds himself in a stressful situation. Give your dog a repertoire of acceptable behaviour that he can use. (See Chapters 6 and 7.) Instead of reacting impulsively to a particular situation, he will learn to act cognitively.

Setting boundaries

Set clear boundaries by giving your dog consistent and accurate feedback about appropriate behaviour. Deal with problem behaviour as described in Chapters 8 and 9. You can use physical boundaries, such as baby gates, to keep your dog out of certain parts of the house. Over time, this response will become conditioned and the dog will likely avoid those areas even without the presence of physical barriers (unless the motivation to enter is extremely high).

Above Manage your dog's access to areas of high value by closing doors from time to time. This helps him to cope on his own when you are not at home.

Consistency

You must be consistent so that your dog can trust you and know what is expected of her. Be consistent in the amount of time you spend with your dog, but also in the way you apply rules and in your expectations. This applies to all household members – if each one of them is setting different standards this can be very confusing for the dog. Come to an agreement

Above Involve the family in resource management so the dog gets consistent feedback. Let your child feed the dog under your supervision.

with the family on how the dog will be dealt with and stick to it. Train your guests too – they must also learn how to respond appropriately (see Chapter 6: Excitement at the door or gate).

Chapter 5

Recognizing stress

Do dogs have emotions?

Yes. Dogs have feelings and thoughts. They can feel scared, angry, anxious, excited and happy. The same chemicals and brain structures that produce emotion in humans are also present in dogs. However, they do not necessarily feel emotions the same way we do. Dogs can sense our feelings and even respond to them, but they probably do not have the ability to imagine what we are thinking.

Humans easily ascribe emotions like jealousy and guilt to dogs, when in fact their dogs are simply responding to things in the environment. A dog that initiates a fight because his owner is giving another dog attention is not jealous; he is merely reacting to what he perceives to be a threat to a valuable resource – his owner's attention. A dog that appears guilty is trying to avoid what it perceives to be an initiation of conflict.

Emotions help animals to adapt to internal or environmental stress. Dogs are constantly exposed to stimuli that cause emotions, which make them behave a certain way. The presence of a threat can cause fear and fearful behaviour, or anger and aggressive behaviour. Fear of an anticipated threat results in anxiety and anxious behaviour, even if the threat itself is not present.

Each dog processes emotions differently – while one dog may find a particular event highly stressful, another dog may not react to it at all. Meeting an unfamiliar person can cause fear in some dogs and excitement in others. How a dog reacts to a stimulus depends on his genetic makeup and what he has learned from past experiences.

The brain and emotions

The brain is made up of millions of cells called neurons. The neurons produce chemicals that affect body functions and behaviour. These chemicals are called neurotransmitters. Serotonin, norepinephrine and dopamine are a few examples of a host of neurotransmitters. An imbalance (an increase or decrease) in neurotransmitters can cause abnormal emotions and behaviour. In people, low serotonin levels are associated with depression. Low serotonin levels in dogs are linked to anxiety, fear and even compulsive behaviour. Different neurotransmitters can play a role in the same type of behaviour; for example, dopamine also affects compulsive behaviour.

Opposite Careful observation of ear position, tail carriage, body posture and eyes can help you gain a better understanding of your dog's intentions and feelings.

Reading your dog's body language

A dog's emotional state is reflected in her body language. By accurately assessing her body language, you can learn more about her state of mind. It will enable you to make better decisions about how to respond to your dog in different situations.

A dog's learning ability is directly linked to her emotional wellbeing. The more relaxed a dog is, the better it will be able to learn. A dog that is fearful, aggressive or anxious will find it very difficult to learn effectively. Successful dog trainers recognize a dog's emotions and accurately predict and modify their actions by paying close attention to the body signals being emitted.

Small changes in a dog's facial expression, posture, tail and ear position, eye orientation and lips can provide valuable information about her state of mind. If we can understand

Above When two dogs greet each other, a multitude of subtle body language changes occur. Note the dog on the left shifting her weight backwards, indicating a non-confrontational approach. The dog on the right has his paw lifted loosely off the ground, also a sign of friendly interaction.

Most drugs used to treat behavioural problems have their effect because they change the levels of one or more neurotransmitters in the brain. While changes in neurotransmitter levels will alter behaviour, the converse is also true: a change in behaviour can effect a change in neurotransmitter levels. This is the basis of behaviour modification – if you can teach the animal with problem behaviour to behave differently in a given situation, the change in behaviour alters the chemical balance in the brain which, in turn, results in sustained normalized behaviour.

The secret to changing a dog's behaviour lies in recognizing his emotions. His behaviour reflects his emotions and, by understanding the type of behaviour that represents a specific emotion, we can address the underlying cause of problem behaviour.

Above Although this dog is barking, the ears pulled back loosely indicate a playful attitude.

more about the complex world of visual signals that dogs use to communicate with each other, we will become more successful at communicating with our dogs.

Dogs use visual signals to reflect their social status and emotions. Social status is either dominant/assertive, submissive/deferent or ambivalent. Emotional signals are indicative of anxiety, fear, anger, confidence or playfulness. The table on page 85 lists some variations of visual signals and provides information on how the dog is feeling at the time. The same signal can have different meanings in different contexts. When interpreting body-language signals, it is important to perceive the dog holistically and not to interpret individual signals in isolation. It is the overall picture and the context in which the dog displays the signals that you must consider when making a decision about a dog's state of mind at a given time.

Not all dogs have the same repertoire of body signals. In many cases their ability to show visual signals has been attenuated. Dogs that were bred for fighting, for example, do not show all the warning signals of aggression, as they were required to initiate a fight quickly without giving their opponent an opportunity to prepare. Other breeds cannot show certain visual signals because they are anatomically incapable of doing so. Dogs with droopy ears are unable to prick their ears, and so the movements of their ears backwards and forwards is much more subtle than those with pricked ears. Curly tails cannot be tucked underneath or wagged profusely; long-coated dogs are unable to show fear and aggression through hair-raising, and their facial expressions are difficult to see.

Top *Note the mild tension in the spaniel's face as shown by the slightly tense skin above his eyes and the straight stare ahead, as he looks at a potential threat.*

Middle *The border collie's face is flaccid, with the mouth open and the body weight shifted backwards, indicating a willingness for friendly interaction.*

Bottom *Once allowed to interact freely, most young dogs will end up playing after a small amount of tension during the initial greeting.*

Body-language interpretation

Submissive dogs wanting to avoid conflict show distance-decreasing signals. These are an invitation to other dogs to approach and an assurance that there is no aggressive intention, as if to say: 'Hi there, let's get to know each other'. Intense distance-decreasing signals can indicate fear or anxiety. Distance-decreasing signals include:

- Play bow
- Relaxed paw lift
- Curved spine
- Ears lowered
- Grinning
- Rolling over
- Low tail carriage or tail wagging wildly
- Body lowered or crouching
- Avoiding eye contact
- Flaccid facial muscles

Calming signals are also distance-decreasing signals, meant to calm both the dog displaying the signal and the one initiating the interaction. Dogs that are feeling anxious or insecure will use calming signals that say, 'I want you to know that I don't want a confrontation, in case that's what you were thinking'. Calming signals include the following:

- Looking away
- Blinking
- Licking the lips or the nose (tongue flick)
- Sitting or lying down
- Sniffing
- Yawning
- Approaching in an arc instead of a direct line
- Sneezing
- Scratching
- Shaking

Top *The play bow signifies a willingness to interact playfully.*

Middle *These tails are carried just above the midline, in a relaxed fashion, signifying positive interaction.*

Bottom *Note the curved spines of both dogs when meeting for the first time and the tucked tail of the young Great Dane. The youngster is submissive towards the elderly bitch. This is appropriate greeting behaviour.*

Interpreting body language

Body part	Variations	Information provided
Body posture	Standing squarely on all four feet, hind feet spread	Confident
	Head lowered	Submissive/deferent
		Guarding
		Playful
		Anxious/insecure
	Neck arched, weight shifted forward	Confident
		Alert
		Challenging
		Dominant/assertive
	Front paw on other dog's shoulders	Dominant/assertive
		Sexual behaviour if bitch on heat
	Body lowered	Relaxed
		Submissive/deferent
	Crouching	Fearful
		Submissive/deferent
	Rolling over, belly exposed	Submissive/deferent
	Stiff stance, spine straight and rigid	Alert
		Dominant/assertive
		Challenging
	Relaxed stance, curved spine (horizontally curved – a C-shape of the spine if viewed from above)	Inviting friendly interaction
	Front paw raised in a relaxed, solicitous manner	Inviting friendly interaction
	Front paw raised in a stiff, definitive manner	Challenging
	Front quarters on ground with hindquarters up (bowing)	Invitation for friendly interaction, so-called 'play bow'
Eyes	Direct gaze	Confident
		Dominant/assertive
		Challenging
	Intense staring, pupils dilated	Challenging
	Looking away/avoiding eye contact	Anxious/insecure
		Submissive deferent
		Fearful
	Blinking	Anxious/insecure
	Eyes narrowed	Anxious/insecure
		Submissive/deferent
Ears	Erect	Alert
		Confident

Body part	Variations	Information provided
Ears	Erect	Confident Dominant/assertive Challenging
	Flattened, pulled back Lowered, flaccid, twisted	Fearful Submissive/deferent Anxious/insecure Playful
Tail	High (above level of back)	Confident Dominant/assertive Challenging
	Low (below level of back, or lower than normal carriage). Note that sight hounds naturally carry their tails low	Anxious/insecure Submissive/deferent Fearful
	Tucked between hind legs	Fearful Submissive/deferent
	Wagging wildly	Excited/playful
	Wagging stiffly, tip only wagging	Challenging
	Stiff and straight	Alert Dominant/assertive Challenging
Lips	Pulled right back as if smiling, corners of mouth relaxed (grinning)	Submissive/deferent
	Pulled back and up, puckered, showing only the incisors and canine teeth (snarling)	Dominant/assertive Challenging
	Pulled back, showing all teeth, corners of the mouth tight	Defensive Fearful
	Licking the lips	Anxious/insecure
	Licking another dog's (or person's) lips	Submissive/deferent
Hair coat	Raised hair (piloerection) right along the back or just on the shoulders and at the tail base	Fearful Anxious/insecure Challenging
Facial expression	Muscles of face flaccid, face smooth	Relaxed Submissive/deferent
	Muscles tense and rigid, frowning, showing ridges or bulges in the skin along the lips, the corners of the mouth and on the muzzle	Challenging Anxious/insecure
	Flared nostrils	Anxious/insecure Fearful Challenging
Movement	Direct approach	Confident Dominant/assertive Challenging
	Curved approach	Invitation for friendly interaction Submissive/deferent
	Freezing – no movement	Fearful

Top *These distance-decreasing signals border on anxiety: note the terrier's curved spine, head held low, flattened ears and the paw lift.*

Middle *Anxiety – the head is turned away but the eyes (showing the white) are oriented towards something the dog is concerned about.*

Bottom *Here the dog is much more relaxed. Her head and eyes face in the same direction, away from the source of concern. The open mouth is also a sign of reduced tension.*

Be aware of over-diagnosing calming signals: all dogs that yawn are not necessarily anxious; the dog may simply be tired. Likewise, sniffing is a normal behaviour in many contexts. The secret is to look at the overall picture, taking into consideration other signals and the physical circumstances.

Behaviour like sniffing, sneezing, scratching and shaking is often referred to as displacement behaviour when it occurs out of context. The behaviour is a substitute for other behaviours when the dog is anxious and not sure what to do; thus the dog scratches where it does not itch or sniffs where there are no smells. As we don't know whether the dog is really itching or picking up a real smell or not, we have to look for other signals and not interpret a displacement behaviour in isolation.

Distance-increasing signals indicate that the dog wants whoever he is interacting with, to stay clear of his personal space. He wishes to increase the distance between himself and what he may perceive as a threat. Distance-increasing signals are meant to avoid conflict, but if the threat persists the dog will be willing and ready to attack. The message is, 'back off, or else'. These signals are warnings of aggressive intent. Dominant/assertive dogs also use distance-increasing signals to assert their social status, often more subtly, conveying the message, 'please get out of my personal space'. Distance-increasing signals include:

- Upright stance, hind feet spread widely
- Neck stiffly arched, spine rigid
- Snarling, showing just the incisors and canine teeth
- Ears cocked

Above *Note the male Labrador's straight body posture, tail held high and raised hair, indicating social assertiveness. The other dog just looks on relaxed, with a slightly curved body.*

Above right *Note how these two dogs shift their weight backwards with friendly playful interaction.*

- Tense facial muscles – clearly defined eyebrows and ridges on the muzzle and along the lips
- Tail up, with or without tip wagging stiffly
- Staring, dilated pupils
- Pilo-erection (raised hair)
- Flared nostrils
- Stiff paw lift

Mixed messages

Fearful dogs show distance-decreasing signals, but in intense fear where the dog is unable to escape from the source of fear, a mixture of distance-increasing and distance-decreasing signals are seen. Defensive dogs also show mixed signals as they are experiencing conflict between anger and fear.

Use your own body language to communicate with dogs

Distance-decreasing signals to reduce anxiety

You can use distance-decreasing signals to assure a dog that you are not a threat. This will be appropriate for interactions with fearful, excessively submissive and anxious dogs.

Do not make direct eye contact, but turn your head away. Approach the dog sideways rather than with the front of your body facing forward. Keep your body low – sit down if need be. Lean back, rather than shift your weight forward. Don't make sudden movements. Wait for the dog to initiate interaction with you. You can even yawn, lick your lips and blink. (There is controversy amongst scientists as to whether or not calming signals really work for dogs if people use them. Most experts agree that they definitely work between dogs. While the jury is still out on this, it certainly won't do any harm for you to use calming signals. After all, other forms of visual communication like avoiding eye contact and shifting body weight certainly do work.)

instead of rushing out). Running away from a dog is more likely to result in the dog coming to you than rushing towards her. Learning dog language means doing a lot of things that are opposite to normal human instinct.

Left The Great Dane uses a relaxed paw lift to initiate play. When people use their hands to shove dogs away, dogs often interpret it as a signal to play.

Use your hips and shoulders

Dogs use their hips and shoulders to control each other's movement. Herding dogs use their bodies in a similar way to move sheep. You can use your body very effectively to control a dog's movements. Exuberant dogs that jump on people respond very well to hip and shoulder movements. If you are standing and the dog jumps up on you, simply fold your arms and turn your back on her, moving your hips and shoulders into her as she jumps. Sitting down, you can also turn your shoulders so that you face away from the dog, or you can lean forward and use your shoulders to block her off. Using your hands to push the dog away will not be effective as most dogs interpret this as an invitation to play, which may be reminiscent of the relaxed paw lift.

Encouraging friendly approaches

Encourage the shy dog to approach you by moving away from her, rather than towards her. Shift your body weight back to convince the dog to come closer, and lean forward to discourage an approach (if you want the dog to stay where she is, for example, wait at the door

Above Use your hips and shoulders to control interaction with a boisterous dog.

How to greet a dog

Normal human greeting behaviour is to approach the other person directly, make eye contact and reach out with a hand to clasp the other person's hand. Very often this is followed by a face-to-face approach for a kiss and embracing each other in a friendly hug.

Because this is how people greet each other, this is how they tend to greet dogs too. Many dogs learn to accept this type of greeting from people they know well, but most dogs interpret such an approach by unfamiliar people as highly challenging (see table below). Depending on how threatened a dog feels about this, its response may vary from mild anxiety, evidenced by calming signals, to extreme arousal, manifested in aggression. This could take the form of a nasty bite on the

How a dog interprets human greetings

What human does	What dog sees	What dog thinks
Walks to dog	*Direct approach*	*Challenge*
Looks at dog	*Direct eye contact*	*Challenge*
Reaches out with hand	*Reaches out with paw*	*Challenge*
Touches dog on head or neck	*Puts paw in my face*	*Challenge*
Holds dog	*Uses paw to restrict my movement*	*Challenge*

Above *When calling a dog that is hesitant to come, lower yourself, present your side to the dog and avoid direct eye contact. This will give the dog more confidence to approach you.*

Above *Note how this border collie hesitates when welcomed with open arms, the owner leaning forward. This is not a dog-friendly way of calling a dog.*

Right Touch a strange dog underneath the chin when you first interact with him or her. Patting a dog on top of the head can be intimidating to the dog.

hand extended so kindly or a bite in the very face offered so lovingly for a kiss and cuddle.

When greeting a dog, be mindful of how the dog interprets your behaviour and keep the following in mind:

• Slow down – approach slowly and in a curve, rather than striding at the dog directly.
• Avoid direct eye contact at first.
• Keep your body low, but don't lean over the dog – rather crouch or sit down.
• Extend your hand so that the dog can sniff first. Offer your hand from below, rather than moving it down from above the level of the dog's head.
• Offer the back of your hand, holding your hand in a loose fist (be sure to protect your fingers!). Ideally, you should have a tasty treat in your hand, so that when you do expose your palm, the dog can discover food there. Keep your palm open for it to eat the treat. This is a good way of gauging how stressed a dog is – if he shows no interest in the treat, he is likely to be fairly stressed, and you will need to slow down your approach even more.
• Breathe normally and watch the dog's breathing pattern – if he takes slow, deep, regular breaths he is probably relaxing. Look out for calming signals and do not force yourself on the dog if he is obviously uncomfortable.

• Only touch the dog once it is relaxed. Touch him first on the chest or underneath the chin.
• Do not hug or kiss dogs unless you know them very well.

Dealing with an approach from an aggressive dog

Be careful with dogs that show aggressive intent – it is best not to approach such a dog unless you are an experienced dog handler. However, if you do find yourself in a situation where an aggressive dog is threatening you, perform the distance-decreasing (friendly) signals described on page 88 and slowly move away from the dog, facing sideways (don't run away). Remember to continue breathing – dogs are very sensitive to this. Keep your arms still at your sides and keep quiet.

Recognizing stress

Dogs show the effects of stress in different ways. If you can recognize stress in your dog, and deal with it correctly, you will not only make it easier for her to learn more effectively, but it will also assist in preventing future behaviour problems. Signs of acute, short-term stress include the physical and behavioural signs listed below.

Physical signs:
- Hyperventilation (breathing fast)
- Hypersalivation (drooling)
- Perspiration: dogs perspire through the skin on their footpads. This is usually visible as sweaty paw prints on smooth surfaces (for example, on the veterinarian's examination table).
- Excessive, sudden hair loss
- Body tension
- Facial tension; for example, ridges formed around the mouth and eyes
- Dilated pupils

Behavioural signs:
- Lack of interest in food treats
- Changes in activity levels: very depressed or excessively active
- Marking behaviour (urinating or defaecating)
- Excessive barking, howling or whining
- Calming signals (page 84)

One or more of these signs may be evident, and the way a particular dog exhibits stress may differ in various environments.

Helping your dog cope with stress

There are three basic steps to follow in dealing with a stressed dog:

- Remove the dog from the stressful situation or remove the stressor.
- Teach the skills required for dealing with stressful stimuli such as relaxation and self-control (see Chapter 6).
- Slowly reintroduce the stressful stimuli (systematic desensitization and counter-conditioning; see Chapter 9).

Opposite These Salukis, although in a potentially stressful show environment, show relaxed body language, reflecting an ability to cope with stress.

Below This dog is showing stress in the presence of a strange dog. She has her mouth wide open in an intense show of submission, showing all her teeth. This is an extreme version of the friendly grin that exposes all the teeth, with long, relaxed lips.

Let's use a common example – the dog that goes to training class for the first time and barks non-stop at the other dogs. She is not interested in treats, toys or her handler; all she can do is look at the other dogs and bark.

First, take the dog away from the other dogs to a distance at which she no longer barks at them and where she is willing to accept rewards. If this means going home, then that's what you must do. The bottom line is – get the dog into a state in which she is capable of thinking and learning.

Then teach her how to relax and exercise self-control. There is no point in addressing a dog's inappropriate stress response if you cannot replace it with an alternative response. This is the part that most people do not address and forms the most important part of

dealing with any stress or anxiety-related behaviour in a dog.

Once she can do the relaxation and self-control exercises well, move her just a tad closer to the other dogs, but stay on the periphery. Repeat the exercises, using ample rewards while you slowly move close to the other dogs, until your dog responds to you in a calm, controlled manner in the presence of other dogs.

Any good trainer knows that successful dog handling requires lots of patience! Do not rush this process; time spent on helping your dog establish a stable internal emotional state is well worthwhile, as it will ensure long-term reliability. Work in short sessions as frequently as possible and set yourself small goals along the way, slowly increasing your expectations as you achieve small victories.

Chapter 6

Teaching life skills

FORMAL DOG TRAINING COURSES OFTEN IGNORE the importance of life skills that help a dog cope in stressful circumstances. A dog with good life skills is predictable, confident and reliable. He gets along with other dogs as well as people, responds appropriately to environmental stimuli and is less likely to develop behavioural problems. Dogs with problems benefit immensely from life skills training, and this should be the first objective of dog training.

The two foundations necessary for good canine life skills are self-control and relaxation. The exercises described in this chapter develop these skills. A relaxed dog is easier to train. When you begin training your dog, ensure that he is relaxed, quiet and breathing slowly, has a relaxed body posture and is sitting or lying with the weight shifted to one side – the so-called 'sloppy' sit or down – focuses on the handler and readily accepts treats.

Start your training in a familiar environment without distractions. Have small, tasty treats ready and do the initial training shortly before feeding, when your dog has an empty stomach and is likely to be more motivated.

Don't be alarmed about teaching 'sloppy' behaviour: we are simply referring to the type of body posture that would promote a calm state of mind. A dog that is sitting or lying straight and symmetrically, with a rigid spine, is more likely to be tense, stressed and poised to react. Relaxation requires a low level of re-activity, so we aim for non-reactive body postures.

You can teach your dog different versions of the same posture for different situations. Sloppy sits and downs are better for stays and settling down, while straight postures work well when you need speed; for example, in a sequence of dance moves.

Remember that your dog is not the only learner. As a trainer you must learn certain skills that you will use every time you teach and train a new behaviour. These are:
- Getting the behaviour without using force. See p97 (Luring and Capturing), p32 and Chapter 7 (Shaping).
- Fading the lure (see p99).
- Achieving fluency (see p98).
- Naming the behaviour or adding the cue (see p99).
- Adding duration (see p104).
- Perfecting the behaviour (see p105).

Most of the exercises in this chapter make use of clicker training (see Chapter 2). You can substitute the clicker for another reward, like a treat or toy, but you will be able to train with more precision and speed using the clicker.

Opposite This dog is alert yet relaxed during training, with a curved spine and neutral tail carriage.

Step 1: Getting the behaviour

a) Luring the sit

Let the dog smell a treat in your hand. Move the treat up in your hand, so that his muzzle follows your hand and his head moves upwards and backwards, until his rump goes down and he sits. If he backs away from you, work against a wall and, if necessary, make a tunnel with chairs so that he cannot deviate.

The idea is not to force the dog to sit by pushing down his rump manually – you want him to sit voluntarily. If he chooses to sit (even if only for a treat) instead of being forced, he will learn more reliably. This may take much patience with an untrained dog, but it is worth the effort. Relaxation has to come from within the dog, it is not something you can force.

Above *It is more difficult for a dog to jump up from the sloppy down than from a straight down.*

Above *The sloppy sit enhances relaxation.*

The instant your dog sits, click and give him the treat. Repeat several times.

b) Capturing the sit

If the dog won't sit when you lure him with a treat, just wait, because at some stage he will sit. Be patient. Then immediately click and treat (capture the sit). Repeat a few times.

Left Hold the treat just above your dog's muzzle. If you hold it too high, he will jump up to grab it.

Above As you move the treat up and backwards, the dog's rump sinks down into the sitting position.

Above *Start using your hand without a treat in it,* *so that the dog will follow your empty hand the* *same way he followed the treat.*

Step 2: Fading the lure

If you did use a treat to lure your dog to sit, the next step is to get him to sit without the lure. Do this by pretending you have a treat in your hand, have the dog follow your hand exactly as before and click the instant his rump hits the ground. Produce a treat from your treat pouch. This reduces the dog's dependency on food. This exercise is called 'fading the lure'. You still give the treat as a reward; you are just not using it as a lure.

Step 3: Fluency

Aim to build up fluency. Fluency refers to your dog offering behaviour without hesitation and luring (see Fading the lure) at least five times in a row. Your dog should demonstrate fluency with any behaviour before you add the cue. You can get more repetitions in a short space of time if you are clever with the delivery of the treat. The sequence is as follows:

- Dog sits
- You click
- You throw the treat on the floor so that the dog has to get up to fetch it. This places the dog in a position to offer the sit again.
- Dog sits
- You click
- Throw the treat
- Dog gets up to fetch the treat
- Dog sits, and so on

Once you have clicked, it doesn't matter if your dog stops sitting, because the click marks and ends the behaviour. What your dog is doing when he gets the treat is not important. The aim is to get several smooth repetitions of the behaviour without hesitation in between the repetitions.

Step 4: Adding the cue

Once the dog sits quickly and willingly, almost obviously asking for a reward, you are ready to add the cue. Do this by saying 'sit' as he puts his rump on the ground. Get the dog into a rhythm of repeating the exercise smoothly a few times without hesitation (build up fluency) in different contexts, then introduce the cue just before it sits.

This is the sequence:

- Dog sits
- You click
- Throw the treat, dog gets up, takes treat
- Say 'sit'
- Dog sits
- Click and throw the treat
- Dog gets up, takes treat
- Say 'sit'
- Dog sits, and so on

You are anticipating the dog's intent to offer the behaviour, and using the cue just as he is about to offer the behaviour. The secret is to get him into a rhythm of repeating the behaviour a few times so that the cue will automatically precede the behaviour.

After several repetitions in a few training sessions, you can just give the cue straight away. Click and treat every time the dog responds correctly to the cue to establish a clear link between the cue, the behaviour and the reward.

Once the dog responds consistently to the cue, you can use the clicker and treats less frequently. Click and treat eight sits out of 10, then six out of 10, and so on until you gradually fade out the clicker and the treat altogether.

Top *The instant the dog sits, you click. This tells the dog that it is the sitting that is being rewarded, and that there is a treat on its way.*
Right *Throw the treat on the ground just in front of the dog, so that he has to get up to eat the treat. Now he is ready for another repetition.*

Step 1: Lure the 'down'

Use a treat to lure your dog into a 'down' position. You can use one or all of three methods:

- Lure the 'down' from a 'sit', by moving the treat down towards the ground, and as the dog lowers his neck and bends his elbows, you move the treat forward along the ground in the shape of an 'L'. Don't move too fast – this exercise takes time! At first, you may just get the elbows to bend – if that's all you get, click and treat it, as it is closer to a 'down' than a sit. (Pictures 1–3)

- Lure the 'down' from a standing position by letting the dog smell the treat in your hand and quickly moving it down onto the ground and between his legs toward his back. As the head drops, he should flop down into a bow position and then drop his hindquarters as well. (Picture 6)

- Lure the 'down' under your legs, or under a coffee table for a large dog. To lure under your legs, sit on the floor with your legs bent slightly, and encourage the dog to follow a treat under your knees to the other side. She should drop her chest onto the ground, followed closely by the hindquarters in her attempt to get through your legs. (Picture 7)

If luring doesn't work, resort to capturing the behaviour: at some point all dogs must lie down.

1–3 Luring the down from a sit. You will click at no 3, followed by a treat.

Catch this moment by clicking and giving a 'jackpot' – an especially nice treat.

Step 2: Fade the lure

Use your empty hand to lure the 'down' as soon as possible. Click and treat every time she offers the behaviour successfully. Gradually use less obvious body movements until you can stand up straight as your dog lies down. (Pictures 4-5)

Step 3: Fluency

Get the dog to do 'push ups': As soon as she lies down, click and treat, putting the treat a foot in front of her so that she has to get up to eat. Aim for five fluent repetitions before adding the cue.

Step 4: Add the cue

As the dog becomes more fluent, say 'down' just before she assumes the position, followed by a click and treat. Repeat many times. Once she makes the association between her chest and hindquarters making contact with the ground, the word 'down' and the reward, she will respond to the verbal cue 'down' by lying down.

4–5 Fading the lure: Use an empty hand and move it behind your back before you click, until the dog is no longer dependent on you bending all the way down.

6 Luring the down from a stand.

7 Use one or both legs to lure the down underneath your legs.

Step 5: Perfect the 'down'

(See Steady Stay, page 104).

Get your dog into a 'sit' or a 'down' and watch his breathing carefully. Wait for the chest to move at regular intervals and for the breathing to slow down if the dog is breathing fast or panting. Click and treat each deep breath. If he is panting, click and treat the first time he closes his mouth. Heat could be the cause of the panting and not just stress, so ensure you are working in a cool environment when doing this exercise.

Make up 10 treats and use them all up in a single 'slow-breathing' session. Once your dog's breathing slows down rapidly and he maintains this rate, you can start adding distractions like people walking past and dogs in the distance. Because the exercise is more difficult, make it easier for your dog to earn a reward – reward more for doing less in a difficult environment.

Above *Slow breathing helps dogs relax and cope better with distractions and stress.*

Combine the 'sit' or 'down' with slow breathing and create a 'settle down' whereby your dog remains quiet and calm in one spot. This is often easier to teach if it is associated with a physical cue like a blanket or mat (generally referred to as a 'settle mat') on which the dog gets used to resting. It provides a visual, physically identifiable area associated with slow breathing and relaxation. Here are two methods that may work for you:

- Ask your dog to sit or lie down on the mat and reward him with a click and treat. After the click, throw the treat next to the mat so that he has to get up to repeat the exercise. Slowly, increase the time period your dog is expected to remain on the settle mat, and then start gradually moving away from it (see pp104–8 for more details).

- Teach your dog to 'go to' the mat. Put the mat down and wait for the dog to look at, sniff or move towards it. Click and treat any interest in the mat. As he shows more interest in the mat, click for him getting on and then lying down or sitting on it. Give the treat off the mat so that he can quickly repeat the action. Move slightly further away from the mat, clicking and treating each time he approaches and gets on it. Once the dog readily gets on his mat from a few metres, reinforce longer 'sits' or 'downs' on the mat (see pp104–8 for more details). You can add the cue 'go to your mat' as soon as he spontaneously offers the behaviour.

Top *Ask your dog to sit on the mat and reinforce longer sits over time.*
Above *Reinforce any interaction with the settle mat to encourage the dog to go to the mat willingly.*

Once your dog understands what 'sit' means, and that it earns rewards, you can develop it further into a 'sit–stay' (and a 'down' into a 'down–stay'). Now, instead of just putting his hindquarters on the floor, he must keep them there.

Making it last longer

To add duration to a behaviour – in other words, to expect your dog to sustain a behaviour for a period of time – is a skill used for many different behaviours. Do so by withholding the click for a few seconds. Ask the dog to sit, and instead of clicking immediately, wait a few seconds and then click and treat. Gradually increase the duration in successive repetitions and randomly. Work at a pace that allows your dog to be successful most of the time. Always come back to something easy when things are going well. The sequence is as follows:

- Ask dog to sit
- Dog sits
- Wait – count 'one potato, two potato, three potato'
- Click and treat
- Repeat, this time waiting two seconds; click and treat
- Repeat, wait five seconds; click and treat
- Wait six seconds; click and treat
- Wait three seconds; click and treat
- Wait four seconds; click and treat
- Wait seven seconds; click and treat

Above *When adding duration to the sit, relax your own body and don't stare at the dog. Sustained eye contact should not be a requirement for the stay – you may want to go out of sight eventually.*

Always end on a high note, when the going is good. In several sessions, build up the duration to 20 or 30 seconds. Make it easy for your dog to succeed and quit while you're ahead.

At this stage, the dog can not only sit on cue, but sustain the sit for a while. However, you want the behaviour even more refined than this. You would like him to sustain the sit as you are moving away from him, in the presence of distractions and even when you are out of sight.

Step 1: Define the behaviour

In order to perfect the stay, you must know exactly what you expect your dog to do: The ideal sit–stay would be for your dog to sit quietly in a relaxed position, for two minutes, while you walk away, moving out of sight briefly, ignoring distractions. Now break it down into its smallest components (criteria):

- Dog puts her hindquarters on the ground
- Maintains a relaxed pose
- Keeps sitting (i.e. duration)
- Sits while you move away
- Sit while you move out of sight
- Sits in the presence of distractions

By now, you should have already achieved the first three objectives. The next step is for your dog to continue sitting as you move away.

Step 2: Add a new criterion

Now add a new criterion – distance (moving away from your dog). When adding distance to the 'stay', forget the fact that the dog can sit for 20 seconds, but work on moving away from him first. Allow your dog to set the pace – you may have to remain at one step for a long time before you can progress to the next step.

- Turn your body, looking away; click and treat.
- Face sideways, shift your weight to the left and to the right; click and treat.
- Shuffle your feet; click and treat.
- Lift up and put down your foot; click and treat.

Above *Adding distance to the stay: At first, simply shuffle your feet and move your body sideways. Reward that a few times before you start taking paces away from the dog.*

- Take one small step sideways and return to your stationary position, click and treat if your dog maintains its position.
- Take two steps sideways; click and treat.
- Slowly increase the size and the number of steps you take sideways, until you can eventually walk in a circle right around the dog while he is sitting still. Click and treat while he maintains the sit as you move around him. You can click while you are at a distance from him, or you can return to him and then click.

Above *Gradually move your body around so that your dog gets used to seeing your back.*

- If the dog breaks the stay before you can click, simply ask her to sit again and make it easier to succeed the next time.
- Once your dog is happy for you to move around her, bring back the time component. Slowly build up the sit to a minute or more, with you moving right around her.
- Increase the size of the circle around her and go briefly out of sight behind a pillar or tree.
- Gradually increase the time spent out of sight by standing behind the pillar or tree.

Step 3: Add distractions

Starting with a five-second sit at a distance of three paces, introduce distractions gradually. Click and treat generously for maintaining the sit in the presence of distractions.

- Start by working far from, but in sight of distractions such as people passing.
- Increase duration to 20 seconds.
- Increase distance to a full circle.
- Gradually move closer to the distractions, back to five seconds and three paces.
- Increase the duration.
- Increase the distance.
- Talk to the people passing, back to five seconds and three paces.
- Increase duration.
- Increase distance.
- Interact with your family, back to basics.
- Increase other criteria.

Summary: Perfecting any behaviour

- You must define it so you know exactly what you are training.
- Break the behaviour down into its smallest components. Identify all the different criteria that you require. From your dog's perspective, what exactly is required?
- Work on one component at a time. Add a new component only when the previous one is offered consistently and confidently at the required level. Increase your standard in tiny steps. Reduce your standard if the dog fails more than three times out of 10.
- Relax your previous criteria when you add a new component. From your dog's point of view, adding a new criterion is like learning a whole new behaviour.

Above *Add a mild distraction once your dog is comfortable with some distance between you and her.*
Drop the standards when you introduce the distraction at first.

- Now combine all the different components. Once the new component is deemed to be of an acceptable standard, incorporate the old criteria one by one until your dog performs them all to your satisfaction. You have now shaped the 'sit' to a 'stay'. If you want to, you can introduce the word 'stay' and/or a hand signal as a cue, or you can

Above *Gradually add more and more distractions.*

simply stick with 'sit'. The dog then learns that 'sit' means 'keep sitting until told what to do next'. You don't have to have a separate cue for 'stay'.

Focus standing still

Take a treat or your dog's favourite toy and move it right up to your face.

- Click as the dog looks at you, and treat.
- Repeat a few times.
- Move your hand with the toy or treat to your face, then move your hand a few centimetres away from your face sideways.
- Click and treat if your dog maintains eye contact and does not follow your hand.
- Slowly move your hand further and further away from your face, until it maintains eye contact no matter where your hand is.
- Continually reward maintained eye contact, until your dog readily maintains eye contact for 10 seconds.
- Add the cue 'look'.

Add distractions gradually. Start with easy ones and build up to more difficult and multiple distractions. This simple exercise can give a dog something to do instead of it being anxious. This helps you control your dog in a highly distracting environment and controls his anxiety or excitement.

Focus on the move

Reinforce the 'look' as above.

- Move one pace forward.
- Click and treat if the dog maintains eye contact while you move forward together.
- Gradually increase the distance you walk while he follows you and maintains eye contact.

Above *Use a toy or treat to get your dog's attention. Reward sustained eye contact.*

- Click and treat every two or three paces. This is the foundation for teaching your dog to walk next to you on the lead.

Life skills exercise no 7: Leave

Dogs love to grab things, particularly tasty things, and then ingest them. For them to learn to 'leave' something highly attractive or appetizing, is quite an exercise in self-control, especially considering their genetic heritage of being natural scavengers. It is, however, a necessity that dogs learn this skill because the things that dogs want to grab are not always healthy and safe. Here are some tips:

- Show the dog a treat in your hand, then conceal the treat in your fist.
- Allow him to try and get the treat, nibble at your fist and paw, but don't open your hand, just hold it still.
- Wait for the dog to give up. The very instant he stops worrying your hand, click and treat. Look for that tiny movement of the head away from your fist, even if it lasts a millisecond. You can give the dog the treat in your fist, or another one from your other hand or treat pouch.

Add the cue 'leave' when the dog consistently leaves your hand alone. Now you can perfect the behaviour:

1 Conceal a treat in your hand and keep it still until the dog loses interest.
2 Click the instant the dog looks away, and give the treat.
3 Perfect the behaviour by placing the treat on the ground. Make it easy to succeed at first.

- Put a treat on the floor, show the dog the treat, and cover it with your hand, foot or an object.
- Say 'leave' and partly expose the treat.
- Click and treat when your dog leaves the treat alone just for a fraction of a second.
- Increase the criteria by rewarding longer periods of withdrawal and exposing more of the treat until it is not necessary to cover it.
- Generalize the behaviour by practising with other items, and in different settings.

Beware: Do not do this exercise with a food-possessive dog until you have implemented resource management (see Chapter 4) effectively for a few weeks, and taught the 'drop' exercise.

'Drop' differs from 'leave' because it refers to dropping something the dog already has in her mouth. This is a useful skill for when your dog has hold of a valuable or dangerous item, and also for taking control of tug toys (see p70).

Here is an easy exercise you can do without the clicker:

- Start with an item that is not too valuable to the dog. She must be quite happy to let go.
- Simply offer a tasty treat as a trade-in for whatever she has in her mouth.
- Say 'drop' as her mouth opens. Repeat until the dog has made the association between the action, the word and the reward.
- Use items that are more valuable to the dog as she learns to respond consistently.
- Make bringing things to you fun for your dog. Even if she is carrying something 'illegal', call her in a friendly manner and reward her for releasing the object, so that she enjoys giving you things.

Below Give your dog a choice between a tasty treat and the toy, and ensure that the treat is more attractive than the toy.

Being able to come when called is a basic requirement for any pet dog. This could be a life-saver one day, but apart from helping to safeguard the dog, it also has deeper behavioural implications: a dog that does not heed the recall considers other things to be more important than responding to his handler. You as the handler should be the most important thing in your dog's life, so that when you call, he drops everything else, no matter how pleasant and interesting it may be. Your dog has to perceive you as being in charge all the time – this gives him security. Managing resources effectively (Chapter 4) plays a very important role in motivating dogs to listen to people.

To teach your dog to come when you call him, ensure that this request always has a positive consequence. Dogs learn from the immediate consequences of their actions, so if your dog does something you don't like and you call him to you to reprimand him, you have effectively taught him not to come when you call, because this action has a negative consequence. Praise and reward him whenever he does come to you, even if he did something wrong shortly before that. It is the coming that will be associated with the positive consequence, not the preceding action. Make informal recalls throughout the day, always rewarding with treats. Have them available on you so that you can reward the dog every single time he comes to you.

If your dog already associates coming to you with negative consequences, completely change

> *Coming when you call should always be fun for your dog*

the context of the recall: change the word you use to call him, your tone of voice and your body language and general attitude, and train in a place where the dog is comfortable.

Ensure that the recall doesn't always signal the end of fun. Dogs learn quickly that the only reason they are called when running off-lead, is to go home. Don't always call him to you when it is time to go; go and fetch him instead. Call him often and let him go again during the walk.

Use your body language to encourage your dog to approach you. Leaning back and moving away is more likely to make him follow you than if you were to move towards him. If your dog is really unwilling to come, make yourself appear smaller by sitting on your haunches or even by lying flat on the ground (my first dog-training instructor made me lie flat, on my tummy). Ensure that you have particularly tasty treats on you to reward the dog when he does come. Work when his stomach is empty just before a mealtime to ensure he is highly motivated by appetite.

If you are afraid that your dog will run off and ignore you completely, use a long lead at first so that you can reel him in towards you while luring him with a treat – no dragging or pulling.

Run back as you reel him in on the long lead. The more you encourage him to repeat the action of coming to you for a reward, the more likely he will be to do it voluntarily. After many repetitions the behaviour will become conditioned (automatic). Conversely, every time he does get the opportunity to run off and ignore you, he will learn that this is what works, and running away will become conditioned. Keep your dog on a lead whenever there is a risk of him not staying safely with you.

Above Hold your dog for a few seconds when he comes to you, and make this pleasant for him.

Make a habit of taking your dog gently by the collar and holding him after he has come to you. Give the dog treats while you are holding him. This will prevent him getting used to coming to you, grabbing a treat and rushing off again. Reward not only the action of coming to you, but also the act of staying with you.

Ideally, begin teaching lead walking off the lead. People tend to become lead-dependent and use it to control their dog, instead of teaching the dog self-control. First, teach your dog to walk next to you. He must learn to focus on you before you start using the lead. When he knows exactly how to do it, adding the lead will be easy. This is because the dog will have learned 'walk' and not 'the faster I can move forward, the better', resulting in pulling on the lead – the most common of training problems.

Start off with the moving-focus exercise described on page 106. Click and treat your dog for remaining in the heel position (next to your knee) while looking at you. The secret is to reinforce this action frequently so that the dog has no time to become interested in anything else. At first, you may only achieve three or four paces of focused heelwork. Whatever you achieve, work on it by slowly increasing the duration of your dog's focus while you are moving.

It is important that the dog should be rewarded during the movement, and not only when you stop. Click and treat on the move as long as the dog continues to maintain heel position. Initially, work in very short sessions. Take lots of play breaks in between the exercises. Over time you can build up to 10 and 20 paces, and start to incorporate left, right and about turns.

The final challenge is to maintain a decent level of focus while on the move, with distractions present. Add distractions slowly and reward the dog more for less when you introduce them. You can also use targeting to teach heelwork (see p134).

1 Reward the dog for looking at you while you are both standing still.

2 Reward the dog for eye contact as you are both moving along.

3 Put the lead on and reward every step that you move forward.

4 Gradually decrease the frequency of rewards so that you click and treat once every few steps.

Dealing with a lead puller

Dogs pull because humans come along! Your powerful pulling pooch must learn that you won't budge if she pulls.

You can certainly deal with pulling without using the clicker and treats. The reward for walking on a loose lead is to go forward (an environmental reward). You can try the following method:

- Stop dead in your tracks the instant the lead tightens and you are no longer in control of the walk. Do not allow your dog to pull you even one centimetre. Plant your feet squarely on the ground and don't budge.

- Wait for the dog to focus on you again, as if to say, 'aren't you coming?'. This may take several minutes – just persist.
- Begin to move forward.
- Repeat until she chooses to walk next to you for several paces.

Instead of standing still, you can also change direction abruptly. Another trick is to make a small circle (with the dog) to get her focus back on you. Your first few walks will not take you much further than a few metres. Just persist, stopping the instant the pulling starts. If you are consistent, the dog will understand.

You can also use rewards by clicking and treating whenever the dog returns and remains in the heel position. Increase the quality and frequency of rewards in the presence of distractions.

If you have a dog that pulls very strongly on the lead, consider the use of a head collar (see Chapter 2). Head collars are designed to fit comfortably and afford you much more control over your dog. They also seem to have a calming effect on dogs. Introduce the head collar gradually. Let your dog wear the collar during feeding and playtime before you attach a lead to the collar.

> *Head collars provide a kind but effective way of controlling a dog that pulls on a lead*

1 Stop the instant pulling starts – plant your feet and do not allow the dog to pull forward.
2 Wait for the moment your dog focuses on you.
3 Walk on only if the lead is slack. Be consistent.
4 If you can anticipate that your dog is about to lose concentration, move unexpectedly into a tight circle to retain her focus.

Your dog should be willing to allow people to touch him, put a collar and lead on him, groom him and examine the different parts of his body. General husbandry like washing, grooming, giving medication and doing a veterinary examination is much easier with a dog that is comfortable with being handled. Such a dog is also much safer around people and less likely to react aggressively to people in his personal space. You are less likely to have problems with an adult dog if you handle him regularly and in a pleasant manner as a puppy. If you handle a dog regularly throughout his life he will maintain a positive attitude to handling.

If your dog is not keen on handling, you will need to desensitize him to it. Do not attempt this on your own if your dog has already attempted to, or succeeded in, biting anybody as a result of being handled. Work with a professional to address the problem correctly.

Certain parts of a dog's body are more sensitive to touch than others. Dogs are usually sensitive about having people touch their feet, heads and mouths. Desensitize the dog by starting with the 'settle-down' exercise described above. Wait for him to relax and start breathing slowly. Touch him on the part of his body that he is least sensitive about. This could be the chest, underneath the chin or on the backline. Touch firmly, as though you are massaging him. Avoid sudden movements and avoid leaning over him at first. Do this exercise in a spacious area where your dog will not feel confined.

Opposite *If your dog is used to being handled, it will be much easier to administer medication.*
Above *If your dog is sensitive to handling, touch her in a non-threatening manner at first. Touch a non-sensitive body part, and do so in a spacious environment without crowding her.*

Reward relaxed behaviour by feeding tasty treats while you touch the dog (a toy or even the clicker may excite him excessively). Then continue the touching/massaging by moving onto the next part of the body, giving treats all the time he remains relaxed. Apply gentle pressure, and if the dog pushes back against your pressure – not flinching – reward him.

Start with short one to two-minute sessions, and gradually build up the duration of the exercise. As he becomes used to being handled on the 'easy' body parts, gradually move onto more difficult areas. Hold a paw for just a second, give a treat, and then slowly increase the duration of paw handling. Expand the handling until you can touch the dog comfortably all over his body while he continues to relax. Move to different locations and try to involve other people to ensure that the dog generalizes his willingness to be handled to all situations.

Jumping to greet

If your dog is like a jack-in-the-box when she greets people, she needs to learn self-control. Ask a helper to assist by acting as an environmental reward – the dog's access to the person becomes her reward for appropriate behaviour. Keep her on the lead and simply don't allow her to approach the person unless she can keep all four feet on the ground. The person helps by withholding all interaction each time the dog loses control. The instant she does so, she also loses the attention of the person. Once the dog can refrain from jumping up, even for just a few seconds, the person

1 Don't allow your dog to make you unpopular because he jumps to greet your friends.

2 The person being greeted must turn away as soon as the dog shows the intention to jump.

3 All social interaction is withheld until the dog has four feet on the ground. This is the moment you would click if you were using the clicker.

4 The dog is rewarded with attention and a treat for remaining controlled during the greeting.

gives her a treat. You can also click when your dog has four feet on the floor, and your assistant can give her the treat. Don't expect too much at first, but build it up over several sessions involving different people. When your dog manages to keep all four feet on the ground, she can graduate to learning to sit or lie down when greeting people.

Excitement at the door or gate

Does your dog rush to the door and launch himself at your guests in excitement? Teach him self-control and relaxation skills at the door. Your goal should be to have the dog sit or lie down quietly when guests arrive until he can tolerate

calm approaches by guests handing out tasty treats. This requires as much guest training as it does dog training.

Step 1: Visitor training

People need to learn that they should not fuel your dog's excitement by talking to or touching him. Instead, they should ignore the dog until he settles down. The dog can get attention, even a treat, from the guest when he is calm, with all four feet on the ground. The instant he gets excited, the visitor must turn and walk away. Generally speaking, the more aloof you are around other people's dogs, the better. You do not have to greet every dog you see – they will not feel offended (though their owners might).

Step 2: Steady-stay on mat with distance and no distractions

Start off teaching greeting behaviour with a 'sit-stay' or 'down-stay'. Choose an appropriate location, in view of the front door or gate, where you would like the dog to stay when guests arrive. Place a settle mat in this position and do the steady-stay exercise, in a 'sit' or 'down' position.

Go through all the steps for a steady-stay (see pp104–8). Increase the duration and then the distance that you move away from the dog to the door.

Left Teach your dog to sit or lie down quietly on a mat a short distance from the door.

Step 3: Steady stay on mat with distractions and no distance

Now, add activity at the door. Start with something mild that will not upset the dog, like a familiar person coming from the inside to open and close the door. You should stay with the dog in his spot and reward him for being calm and not leaving the settle mat. Click and treat repeatedly for relaxed behaviour.

Add more activity at the door: for example laughter and animated conversation. Then have a real visitor stand at the open door for just a moment and move on. Reward the dog for not rushing to the door. Ask the visitor to stay a little and chat. Ask the visitor to talk and walk over the threshold. Next time the visitor can come in two paces, and so on. All the time reward the dog for calm behaviour.

Step 4: Steady stay on mat with distance and distractions

Once the dog can tolerate a reasonable level of activity at the door, start working on moving away from him and to the door. Do this with mild activity at the door to start with (remember to relax previous standards when adding something new).

Gradually build up to the real situation by frequently rewarding the dog for staying calm. If he loses control, calmly return him to the mat and repeat the exercise, making it a little easier this time. This exercise is likely to take several training sessions. Be patient, and generous with rewards.

Above Do not expect your dog to endure the actual arrival of guests unless you have gradually built up her coping skills.

Fear of greeting strangers

A dog that feels threatened by advances from strangers must become more confident. Let the dog associate strangers with fun – play a fun game with the dog in the park with strangers walking past, or when you have visitors. Once she is relaxed, invite people to join in the fun. Have strangers throw a ball or present the dog with her favourite toy. It is fine if the dog returns the ball to you and not the other person – it will take a while until she plucks up the courage to initiate interaction with strangers. You can also ask strangers to feed her treats, as long as she remains relaxed.

Teach the dog to sit or lie down when strangers approach. Reward her for sitting calmly when strangers walk past her, and especially when they walk up to her and touch her. Use hand targeting (see p133) to encourage the dog to approach people. Observe its body language carefully; calming signals indicate a low level of stress (see Chapter 5). If calming signals persist or develop into distance-increasing signals, you need to stop the interaction immediately. In such cases, it is too risky and will require a controlled desensitization and counter-conditioning programme (see Chapter 9).

Above *Hand targeting is an excellent tool for the dog that is nervous of strangers. If it starts off as a fun exercise, and touching strangers' hands is made worthwhile (rewarded), it will make him more confident with strangers.*

Problems with dogs greeting dogs fall into two major categories: the over-exuberant, excessively playful dog and the dog that reacts with fear or aggression to other dogs.

Aggression or enthusiasm

Sometimes it is difficult to distinguish between enthusiasm and aggression. Dog handlers often exacerbate interdog problems by the way they react when their dog meets others: the dog sees another dog and wants to greet it, but the handler is afraid that a fight might ensue and instinctively jerks the dog back, reprimanding him. This makes it impossible for the dog to

Above Dogs meeting dogs can and should occur without stress.

explore social relationships and to develop social skills. In addition, he begins to associate other dogs with unpleasant things and learns to be apprehensive of them. Dogs can also sense our own tension when a strange dog approaches. This tension is conveyed to the dog and reinforces this fear. If dogs were allowed to interact freely one on one, chances are there would be very few fights because most dogs inherently want to avoid them.

Learning social skills

Early appropriate socialization with other dogs will prevent most aggression problems between unfamiliar dogs. Many dogs, however, have not been properly socialized, or have even had traumatic experiences with other dogs and do not have the social skills to interact appropriately with strange dogs.

Lack of social skills among dogs manifests as fear, aggression or uncontrollability. The fearful or aggressive dog must learn how to relax, and the uncontrollable dog must learn self-control to interact more appropriately with other dogs. (Refer to the section on 'Helping your dog cope with stress' in Chapter 5.) Set up situations where you can control your dog's

Above You can prevent aggression between dogs from different households by allowing free social interaction from an early age. Control dogs during free interaction by recalling them from time to time.

exposure to other dogs and encourage him to exercise self-control and relax in the presence of other dogs by rewarding relaxed, controlled behaviour. Start off with easy situations and gradually build up to more difficult interactions. Unfortunately, there is no quick fix – only patience and lots of repeated, controlled exposure will remedy the problem of poor interdog social skills (see p182).

Do not let go of the lead unless you are sure that you can control your dog. Beware, though, of reinforcing apprehension by pulling the lead tightly every time you see strange dogs. Keep a safe distance from them, but keep the lead slack. Maintain a happy-go-lucky attitude when passing or meeting other dogs – it will eventually rub off on your dog.

Letting go of the lead when a fight starts

This technique is appropriate for young dogs that are mildly reactive to other dogs. Dogs with severe fear or aggression towards other dogs should be dealt with as described above.

Being on a lead gives a false sense of security to dogs that already view other dogs with apprehension. They sense 'support' at the other end of the lead. This makes them act meaner than they would have had they been on their own. For this reason, dog-training instructors often advise handlers to drop the lead on the ground and walk away when their dog acts aggressively towards another dog. This technique can be very effective, as the dog suddenly realizes that he is not simply the extension of the lead and owner, but that he has to fend for himself. In most cases, the dogs interact appropriately without aggression. However, it is advisable not to try this without an experienced dog trainer's assistance and in a safe environment, as there is a risk involved if the other dog has poor social skills.

Below The handler of the white German Shepherd simply drops the lead and walks away when her dog reacts aggressively to the Border collie. No fight ensues.

Chapter 7

Teaching practical skills

TRAINING ENHANCES MENTAL WELLBEING BY providing mental stimulation. It gives dogs something constructive to do, not only during formal training sessions, but also when they may be faced with unfamiliar circumstances. A trained dog is more likely to respond with appropriate behaviour in a difficult situation than an untrained dog that may respond emotionally rather than cognitively. Training, in particular operant training, teaches a dog to think before doing things and not just to react to stimuli.

In this chapter, we cover some of the more practical, fun skills that will enable you and your dog to enjoy each other's company and even entertain friends.

The focus is not on producing show-quality behaviour, but on simply exposing you to some ideas for training. You will therefore have a variety of behaviours you can work on during your training sessions. Work through Chapter 6 first with particular emphasis on the following steps:

- Getting the behaviour without forcing it
- Building up fluency
- Adding the cue
- Adding duration
- Perfecting the behaviour

Turn to page 43 for more detailed information on clicker training. As before, if you prefer not to use a clicker, simply replace the click with a food treat or other reward.

Most of the exercises in this chapter are shaping exercises (see p32). In practical terms it means rewarding the dog initially for very small steps towards the final behaviour. Anything that remotely resembles the final behaviour should be rewarded. When the dog starts repeating the action voluntarily, you can reinforce more difficult versions until you achieve the final trick.

Building fluency

The most common reason for failure is that we expect too much too soon. Build up each new trick in tiny steps, rewarding each step generously. The more frequent the rewards, the faster the dog learns. Aim for fluency – as soon as the dog is in a rhythm of repeating the same action fluently and without hesitation, you are ready to take it a step further.

Use the ideas on these pages to spice up your training sessions. Think up your own tricks and watch your dog carefully for new behaviours that you can capture. Be creative, allow your dog to be creative and enjoy the process!

Opposite *Targeting (touching a target such as the tip of a stick) is a skill that can be applied to teach many tricks and useful behaviours.*

Make your own target stick (a dowel with coloured tape on one end) or buy a custom made one. The idea is for the dog to nudge or touch the tip of the target stick with its nose. Hold the target stick and clicker in the same hand, so that you can use your other hand to dispense treats. Present the stick to your dog, a few centimetres from its nose.

- Click and treat when he touches the tip or moves towards it with his nose. Hold the target stick still.
- Hold the stick a little further away and reward bigger movements towards the stick.
- Move the stick up high and down low, left and right and reward touches in different positions.
- Move the stick about 10 centimetres. Click and treat each time your dog follows the stick.
- Add the cue 'touch'.

Transfer the behaviour to other targets, such as a plastic lid, a toy or your hand. Present the new object, ask the dog to 'touch'; click and treat any nose touches. If your dog shows no interest in the target, dab a little peanut butter on the end. If he bites the target stick instead of touching it, click a bit sooner before he makes contact with the stick. Concentrate on clicking for the movement towards the target, rather than the actual touch. There are many other applications of targeting – from teaching your dog social skills to entertaining tricks. Read on!

Top *You can make your own target stick by painting or taping the tip of a dowel.*

Middle *Telescoping pointers make excellent target sticks.*

Bottom *Some dogs do better with a visible target on the end of the stick.*

1 Click the instant the dog touches the tip of the target stick.

2 Hold the target stick and clicker in one hand; feed treats from the other hand.

3 Once the dog repeatedly touches the target, start moving the target for him to follow it.

4 After adding the cue, transfer the cue to another object, such as a plastic lid.

Above *Hold a treat between your fingers to encourage hand targeting.*

Teach your dog to touch a hand that is held in front of her. If your dog already knows the 'touch', simply present your hand and ask her to 'touch'. Click and treat any touches or movements towards it. Present both the palm and back of your hand. If this is a new behaviour for the dog, proceed as follows:

- Put a treat between your middle and ring finger and present your hand to the dog.
- Click as he nudges your hand, and let him have the treat.
- Repeat a few times.
- Now present your hand without a treat. Click and treat any touches.
- Present both your palm and the back of your hand. Click and treat all touches.
- Move your hand to different positions and click and treat all touches.
- Add the cue 'touch'.

Hand targeting for shy dogs

Hand targeting is a particularly useful technique in helping shy dogs deal with approaches from strangers. The dog is rewarded for touching a presented hand, making him more willing to approach people.

Ask someone your dog knows to present the back of their hand, first with a treat and then without. Ask your dog to 'touch' and reward generously when she does. Once she is comfortable with people she knows, move on to unfamiliar people. Ask them not to pat or touch the dog, just present their hand, until she is comfortable with them.

Below: *Click the instant the dog touches your hand.*

Fun exercise no 3: Improve heelwork with targeting

You can use either stick or hand targeting to encourage your dog to walk next to you on the lead. Hold the stick in front of the dog's nose (particularly useful for small dogs as it prevents you from having to walk with a bent back), or your hand at your side, and ask it to 'touch' as you move forward. Click and treat every few paces as it remains in the heel position.

Left *Teach your dog to walk in the heel position by following the target stick.*
Below *You can use your hand as a target to encourage your dog to walk at heel.*

Start with a plastic pole or pipe lying on the ground. Use safe, light equipment.

- Use the target stick to guide your dog over the pole.
- Click as he lifts his front feet to clear the pole.
- Throw the treat on the floor in front of the jump.
- Encourage him to jump straight over the pole, without turning or twisting – you don't want your new star to suffer from a sports injury!
- Lift the pole slightly, just a few centimetres off the ground. Repeat the exercise. Click as he starts to jump.

- Gradually fade out the target stick by making it shorter and shorter, until your hand gesture alone provides the cue for jumping. You can combine this with a verbal cue if you wish – change from 'touch' to something else, for example 'over' (how to change cues is described on page 144).
- Young growing dogs (up to a year old) should not jump higher than elbow height. Excessive exercise can damage the growth plates in their bones and joints.

1 Click as the dog crosses the jumping pole.

2 Throw the treat to the front of the jump to maintain forward momentum.

3 Once the dog is comfortable jumping over the pole, raise it slightly.

4 Raise the height of the jump in very small steps.

Use your hand as a target. Hold it just above the dog's head and ask for a touch. Click and treat. Lift your hand and reinforce higher and well-controlled jumps (how high will depend on the size of your dog). Eventually your upraised hand will be the cue for jumping up. You can add a verbal cue by changing the cue

Above *You can teach 'jump for joy' using your hand as a target or the target stick.*

'touch' to something else, and then gradually fade out the hand signal. This exercise is not for dogs with arthritis or hip problems!

To get the dog to spin in a tight circle on the spot, ask her to touch the stick as you move it in front of her nose in a circular movement. Click first for quarter circles, then for half circles until she does a full circle. Over time, you can shorten the target stick and fade it out completely and add a verbal cue, or use a hand signal.

Above *Move the target stick just a fraction sideways to initiate the twirl.*

Start by clicking for a few sits. Then hold the target stick just above nose level, while the dog is still sitting. Ask him to touch. He must stretch his neck to touch the stick. Click and treat for stretching first, then for the slightest movement of the front feet off the ground. Gradually refine the movement to a perfect 'beg'. Change the cue to 'say please'.

Above *Use the target stick in a controlled upwards movement to elicit the 'beg'.*

Stand in front of the dog with your right leg extended forward, bent at the knee. Now use the following sequence:

- Use a treat or target stick in your right hand to lure the dog between your legs, from the inside out.
- Click as she passes between your legs.
- Throw the treat on the floor just ahead of your foot, to encourage her to turn back for the next weave.
- Repeat on one side until she does it fluently.
- Do the same exercise, this time moving her out behind your left leg to the left side, until this is fluent.
- Now combine the right and left weave. Guide the dog through a right weave. As she exits, move your left leg forward. Click and treat as she enters behind your left leg. Use the placement of the treat to ensure that the dog completes the move by bending around your left leg to the inside again.
- You can add a cue 'weave', but by this time the dog usually responds to the position of your legs and hands as a visual cue for the behaviour.
- Take more and more steps as the two of you become more fluent.

1 Hold the target stick just outside your knee and ask the dog to 'touch'.
2 Move the target stick slightly forward and click for the movement towards the target.
3 Throw the treat in front of your foot to encourage the dog to move around your foot inwards. Repeat 1–3 several times until the dog is fluent with that side.
4 Repeat the same exercise on the other side.
5 Place the treat in the path you want the dog to follow.

Teach your dog to be a soccer player by pushing a ball with its nose. Put down a ball in front of it. Ask the dog to touch the ball, and click and treat if he does. If he doesn't, click and treat any interaction with the ball: for example looking at the ball, then sniffing it and then touching it. Once the dog is comfortable touching the ball, reinforce only the harder touches, until he can actually push the ball over a distance. Teach him to push the ball into a box lying on its side. Change the cue to 'score a goal!' or 'Beckham!'

Below Start the exercise by reinforcing any nose touches to the ball.

Transfer the 'touch' to a plastic lid. Initially hold the lid in your hand, near floor level. Then put it down on the floor and click and treat touches. If the dog doesn't want to touch at all when you are no longer holding the target in your hand, you need to take more time to wean him off the proximity of your hand to the target. Increase the distance between your hand and the target very slowly. Now stick it to the wall just off the ground, and repeat until the dog is comfortable targeting the object without you holding it, in a vertical position on the wall.

- Stick the target onto a closed cupboard door.
- Click and treat a few touches.
- Open and close the door a few times to get the dog used to the sound.
- Open the door slightly and reinforce a few touches.
- Click only for harder pushes to close the door.
- Repeat with the door slightly more open.
- Repeat the process until she comfortably closes the door with hard pushes.
- Slowly make the target smaller until she closes the door without the visible target.
- Change the cue to 'close the door'.

Above left Hold the target on the door and ask the dog to 'touch', then gradually move your hand further and further away.

Above right Click and treat for touches on the plastic target on the closed cupboard door.

Changing a cue

Change a cue by preceding the old cue with the new one. Give the new cue, then the old one and click and treat when your dog responds correctly. Eventually you can drop the old cue. The sequence is as follows:

- Say 'close the door'
- Say 'touch'
- She closes the door.
- Click and treat

- Repeat several times
- Say 'close the door'
- She closes the door
- Click and treat
- Repeat several times

> *Changing a cue: New cue, old cue, click and treat.*

Above left *Open the door slightly and reinforce touches on the target.*

Above right *Gradually make the target smaller until she pushes the door without any target.*

Would you like to be able to send your dog to a spot a few metres away and ask him to lie down there and stay? Then try the following.

Step 1

You can use one of two methods:

- Plant the target stick upright in the ground. Ask the dog to 'touch', and point towards the target stick. Click and treat every touch. (Picture 2)

- Transfer targeting to a plastic lid. Hold the lid in front of the dog's nose, just above the ground. Ask him to 'touch' and click and treat. Now put it down on the ground, ask him to touch and reward. Gradually move your hand further away from the target. Repeat a few times until he is confident with touching the lid when it is in different places.

Step 2

Now move one pace away from the target stick or lid. Repeat the exercise a few times. Use a sweeping movement of your hand towards the target together with the verbal cue 'touch'. Click and treat touches. Gradually move the target further away until he moves away from you towards the target every time.

1 Plant the target stick upright in soft soil, or use another target that you can put down on the ground.

2 Click and treat as the dog touches the tip of the target stick.

Step 3

As a separate exercise, teach the dog to lie down after touching the target. The 'down' needs to be on cue before you can proceed any further. Stand right next to the target. Ask her to touch, then ask for a 'down' immediately after she has touched. Click and treat for the 'down', not the touch. Repeat the 'touch–down' several times.

Step 4

Add distance again gradually: Ask her to 'touch' and 'down' while you slowly increase the distance between you and the target. Soon you will have combined the send–away with the touch–down and should be able to send her away to the target and instruct her to lie down from a distance.

Step 5

Make the stick progressively shorter, or the lid progressively smaller until the dog will go in whatever direction you point when you say 'touch', without the visible target. Very impressive! Finally, you can change the cue 'touch' to 'go away' (see p144).

3 Teach the dog to touch the stick and then lie down ('touch', then 'down'). Click when he lies down and give a treat.

4 Once he has mastered the 'touch' followed by 'down', gradually move further away from the target.

5 Now you can control your dog over a distance by sending him away to lie down at the spot you determine.

1 Move a concealed treat sideways so that the dog has to shift her weight as she sniffs it. Click the instant one paw lifts slightly off the ground.

2 Click for higher paw lifts until she paws your hand.

3 Open your hand as if in a handshake.

To get your dog to give you a paw, follow this sequence:

- Show your dog a treat and conceal it in your fist. Hold your hand just below her muzzle. This is usually easier with the dog sitting.
- Wait for your dog to nudge and paw at your hand in an attempt to obtain the treat.
- Click and treat any paw movement towards your hand, even if it is a small movement at first.

- Reward higher, and more controlled paw movements in subsequent repetitions.
- Omit the treat in your hand.
- Open up your palm in a true handshake.
- Add the cue 'hello!' or 'give a paw!'

- Click for 'give a paw' a few times.
- Hold your hand higher.
- Selectively click for higher paw movements only.
- Change the cue from a handshake hand to a 'high five' hand.
- Add the verbal cue 'high five!'

Top *Reinforce higher paw movements.*

Above *Move your hand with the fingers facing upwards to become the visual cue for 'high five'.*

Fun exercise no 14: Wave

To get your dog to 'wave', start off with a few 'high fives'. Then follow this sequence:

- Move your hand away just before the dog touches it.
- Click the paw movement as he paws thin air.

- Now click only for multiple paw movements in the air.
- Gradually reduce your hand movement and introduce a new cue for the wave, for example 'bye-bye!'

Above *Click and treat for sustained and multiple paw movements to elicit the wave.*

Paw targeting is useful for agility training and many tricks. It can even be used to train the paw-give, high five and wave. Use the following sequence:

- Put a target object on the floor and hide a treat under it, or hold it in your hand with a treat in the same hand.
- You can use a plastic lid, but it must look different to any other target you may use for nose targeting.
- Wait patiently until the dog touches the object with his paw as he tries to obtain the treat.
- Click and treat any paw movement towards the object until the dog's paw movements become more purposeful.
- Click only for full paw contact.
- Move the target around.
- Add a cue like 'paw' or anything that doesn't sound too similar to an existing cue.

Above right *Click for pawing at the target object on the floor.*

Right *Pick up the object in your hands and reward all paw touches.*

Backing off can be a very useful behaviour if, for example, there is broken glass on the floor and you want the dog to keep a distance. Use the placement of the treat to your advantage in this exercise. The sequence is as follows:

Above You can also teach your dog to back off by using a target stick.

- Sit on a chair.
- Put a treat between your feet.
- Let the dog take the treat.
- As she looks up at you for another treat, her weight will shift backwards.
- Click the shifting of the weight.
- Put the treat between your feet again.
- Repeat a few times.
- Hold out the click for one step backwards (usually with one of the hind legs).
- Click for any movement backwards. After each click, return it to the same position by placing the treat between your feet.
- Click for more steps backwards.
- Once the dog can take several steps backwards, start clicking for when she moves in a straight line.
- Add the cue 'back off' with or without a hand signal.
- Change your position to standing and drop your standards initially by clicking for small backward movements until the dog gets the idea again.

To get the dog to roll over, start by asking him for a sloppy down.

- Use the treat to move his muzzle sideways and up (a circular movement sideways and then backwards), bending his neck so that he flops over on his side.
- Click and treat for bending the neck first, then for flopping on his side.
- Once the dog is on its side continue the movement over towards the other side.
- Click and treat as he rolls over.
- Add the cue.

1 Starting from the 'down' position, use a treat to lure the dog to bend right over backwards.

2 At first, click and treat for any action vaguely resembling the full roll-over.

3 Take the behaviour forward one step at a time until the dog is smooth in her movement.

The initial part of the roll over, flopping down onto the side, can be taught as a separate behaviour. Click and treat for lying on the side.

Add duration and then the cue 'pass out', and use it as a fun substitute behaviour for jumping on people.

Above *Click the instant the dog flops over, and give a treat.*

As you lure your dog into a roll over (see p152), you can also arrest the movement when he lies on his back. Click and treat the dog as he is lying on his back. Reward any longer duration of this behaviour and then add the cue 'play dead'.

Above *Use a lure, as for the roll-over, to get the dog onto her back. Click and treat initially just for attaining the position, then add duration.*

You can teach the dog to put her chin on the ground and keep it there, looking very tired indeed. It is best if you do this exercise at the end of your training session, or after physical exercise when the dog is likely to be tired already. This is the sequence to follow:

- Ask her to lie down.

- Click and treat any downward movement of the head.
- Now click and treat only when the dog's chin touches the floor.
- Add duration.
- Finally, add a cue 'are you tired?'

Above *Click the instant the dog's chin touches the ground, then give a treat. She will learn quickly what she has to do to earn another reward.*

Chapter **8**

Management solutions

Dogs present with a variety of behaviour problems. You can address many of these with simple, common-sense solutions. Lots of so-called problem dogs are simply bored, and become exemplary as soon as they receive more mental and physical stimulation. Often, it is a matter of a dog having learned the wrong behaviour; all you need do is re-teach acceptable behaviour. Other cases are more complicated and difficult to fix, and may require a combination of behaviour therapy techniques, which may even include medication.

In this chapter we will discuss problems that are more of a nuisance than an abnormality – for example, digging and barking. In Chapter 9 we will look at more serious and complex problems, such as aggression and phobias. Many behavioural problems may overlap and fall into both these categories, but for practical purposes this categorization distinguishes between those requiring a straightforward approach and others that are more complex to treat.

The three main approaches to nuisance behaviour are: relieving boredom, making the environment more conducive to good behaviour and re-teaching appropriate behaviour.

Relieving boredom

Dogs that are bored are dogs that 'self-employ'; there is nothing interesting to do, so they find things to amuse themselves. This is common in young dogs (up to two years of age) and in puppies that are teething (two to four months old).

These dogs need more physical stimulation in the form of exercise, more mental stimulation in the form of structured interaction, including training and walks, and an enriched environment (see Chapter 3). Examples of behaviour that may be the result of boredom are destructive activities such as chewing and digging, and barking and howling.

Modifying the environment

When you are not present to supervise your dog, you need to find ways of encouraging him or her to behave appropriately. Different behaviours require different approaches, but in general you should provide your dog with access to appropriate, attractive opportunities to express his or her needs and deny them access to problem areas, or make these less attractive. Modifying the environment can be useful in counteracting digging, rubbish raiding, stealing from countertops and escaping.

Opposite Certain breeds, and some individuals, need high levels of physical and mental stimulation. This border collie is playing flyball: the dog pushes the carpeted platform to release a tennis ball, which must be caught and taken back to the handler over several jumps.

RE-TEACHING

Re-teaching comprises identifying and removing the reinforcement for attention-seeking and unruly behaviour that occurs in your presence and, if necessary, interrupting and replacing it with an appropriate activity. The steps involved are described in this section.

Step 1: Identify and remove the reinforcement

Above *Avoid problem behaviour if your dog gets overexcited when visitors arrive. Keep him controlled on a lead so that he can't be successful with unwanted behaviour.*

A dog will only repeat behaviour if it is rewarding. If a behaviour that was reinforced is no longer reinforced, the dog will stop doing it. This process of 'unconditioning' is called extinction. When extinction is used to stop a behaviour, the behaviour may get worse before it gets better. This is called the 'extinction burst'.

You can stop your dog performing undesired behaviour if you never again reward it. Try to ascertain what makes a particular behaviour rewarding – is it social interaction, access to food or a toy, or motivating environmental stimuli? Once you have identified the reward, find a way of withholding it. Refer to the table on the opposite page for examples of behaviour reinforcement and how to remedy the associated nuisance behaviour.

The use of extinction to deal with nuisance behaviour

There are two potential problems with extinction: firstly, the dog is not taught an acceptable alternative behaviour and then replaces the behaviour with another unacceptable behaviour. Extinction can only be effective when combined with reinforcement of another,

Identifying and removing the reinforcement

Behaviour	Possible reinforcement	How to effect extinction
Jumping on people	Attention, physical interaction, touch, verbal interaction, eye contact	Keep hands off the dog Turn away from the dog Keep quiet Look the other way
Grabbing a forbidden item and running off	Getting a chase game	Don't chase the dog Trade the item for something more valuable, e.g. food treat
Whining at the door to be let in	The door opens access to preferred location	Do not open the door when the dog whines Open the door when whining stops Anticipate and open the door before whining starts
Shredding the rubbish bag	Food scraps inside the bag	Put the rubbish bag out of reach

desirable behaviour (see p161). Secondly, in the process of extinction, the extinction burst may create the incorrect impression that the problem has not been resolved.

Let's look at an example: your dog is used to being petted every time she jumps on you. Now you keep your arms folded and turn your back when she jumps. She jumps again, and again. She paws at you, whines and launches herself at you like a missile. You remain a pillar of disinterest. She gives up.

If she did get attention while intensifying the behaviour – namely, during the extinction burst – you would have strongly reinforced the intensified behaviour. The dog would have learned that trying really hard does work. Be prepared for the extinction burst when you are dealing with an undesirable behaviour and make sure that you don't reinforce it – ever!

Above Always wait for your dog to be calm before you open a door for him. Never open a door to a whining or scratching puppy – this simply reinforces the nuisance behaviour.

Sometimes, no matter how hard you try not to reinforce unwanted behaviour, your dog keeps on doing it. Every time he initiates and completes an unwanted behaviour, that behaviour is reinforced. If you can interrupt the activity successfully, your dog will be less likely to repeat it.

***Above** Be ready to interrupt unwanted behaviour the instant it occurs.*

You should interrupt the behaviour without causing your dog fear or pain. A tin with coins inside it (shake can), a water pistol or a party horn can make good interrupters. Sound-sensitive dogs (certain individual dogs and often Border collies) may find the noise of the shake-can distressing. In this instance, a squirt of water may be more effective, but for some dogs (especially water-loving dogs such as Labradors) it may actually reinforce their behaviour. In this instance, add a few drops of citronella oil to the water to make it less appealing. It is better if the interrupter is not directly linked to a person, so do not use your voice, for example, as your dog could miscon-strue this as verbal reinforcement.

Interruption is effective only if it is delivered the moment the unwanted behaviour occurs. Remember, dogs can only learn from the immediate results of their actions. With interruption, just as with extinction, it is essential that you teach your dog another, acceptable behaviour so that she has something familiar to default to in such a case. First teach the new, acceptable behaviour and then use it in conjunction with interruption to replace unwanted behaviour.

> *Use interruption only if extinction is not successful*

Step 3: Teach a substitute behaviour

Substitute behaviours

Unwanted behaviour (what you don't like)	Substitute behaviour (what you do like)
Dog jumps up on people	*Dog keeps all four feet on the ground*
Dog barks at the window	*Dog chews toys*
Dog rushes to the door when the doorbell rings	*Dog sits on its mat in the kitchen*
Dog nips at visitor's clothes	*Dog carries toy in mouth when visitors arrive*
Dog mounts person's leg	*Dog lies down on mat*

Even if you have removed the reinforcement for unwanted behaviour successfully or are able to interrupt it, you still need to teach substitute behaviour. If you don't, the behaviour may resurface later or another problem behaviour could develop in its place.

Focus on the positive rather than the negative: if your dog does something you don't like, don't focus on telling the dog what not to do; he is much better at doing things. Think about what you want him to do, not what you don't want him to do. Encourage an alternative behaviour that is incompatible with the problem behaviour, and reward it, so that the alternative behaviour becomes conditioned.

Instead of focusing on stopping the dog from nipping people, focus on getting him to carry his toy around and reward him for that. Instead of stopping him rushing to the door when the doorbell rings, make sitting on the mat more worthwhile. Teach your dog an appropriate new behaviour to replace an existing inappropriate one. The relaxation and self-control exercises described in Chapter 6 are all good substitute behaviours.

Above *The dog has learned to lie down quietly instead of helping herself to food.*

Above *Trying to deal with a boisterous dog when you are arriving home from work will not be successful. Try to avoid such a situation.*

Above *Set up the greeting when you have had time to get out of your working clothes and have the treats and interrupter ready.*

Set the stage

When dealing with problem behaviour that requires re-teaching through extinction, interruption and replacement, it is wise to plan your training sessions carefully. You will not get positive results quickly if you try to deal with the problem as it occurs. If your dog jumps on you every time you return from work with your briefcase in one hand and shopping bag in the other, and you are tired from a long day at work or school, chances are you will not be able to deal with the situation successfully.

Rather, get someone to hold the dog on a lead on your arrival, or put her in a place where she doesn't have direct access to you. Organize your training session for when you are well prepared, wearing old clothes, rested and calm.

- First teach the substitute behaviour – sitting on a mat, for example (see Chapter 6) by repeatedly rewarding it. Work initially in a calm, quiet environment where the dog will not be distracted easily.
- Have an interrupter and some rewards ready. Make sure the rewards are sufficiently motivating and that the interrupter works for the dog.
- Set up a situation that is similar to the context in which the problem behaviour occurs, and encourage this behaviour (jumping, in this instance).
- Interrupt the problem behaviour the instant it starts. Timing is of the essence! It often helps to have an assistant; one person does the interrupting while the other does the rewarding. Switch roles regularly.
- Request the substitute behaviour and reward that.
- Repeat a few times, and then repeat the whole exercise in a different location or with different people.

Dealing with specific problems

Nuisance behaviour that occurs when a dog is alone (destructiveness or digging) can often be resolved simply by providing more physical and mental stimulation to relieve boredom. When problem behaviour is directed at people (jumping up or nipping), it is usually a form of attention-seeking that requires immediate attention.

Excessive attention-seeking behaviour

Dealing correctly with attention-seeking behaviour is one of the cornerstones of behavioural therapy. Most uncontrollable or 'stubborn' dogs are excessive attention seekers and respond well to non-reinforcement and being taught appropriate substitute behaviour. Examples of attention-seeking behaviour are:

- Jumping
- Pawing
- Mouthing
- Nipping (at limbs or clothes)
- Jumping on worktops and stealing food
- Grabbing and chewing objects
- Mounting
- Masturbation

Dogs with high attention needs are either getting too much uncontrolled attention or not enough quality attention. Address the underlying problem by ensuring that you regularly spend structured quality time on your terms with your dog (see Chapter 4). Mounting and masturbation are normal canine behaviours that can occur in males and females, neutered and unneutered. Castration usually causes a significant decrease in mounting behaviour.

Above *Learn to ignore excessive attention-seeking behaviour by withholding all social interaction with the dog.*
Below *Teach your dog an appropriate substitute behaviour, such as lying on a mat chewing a chew toy.*

Destructive behaviour

Boredom, attention seeking and anxiety can cause destructive behaviour. Young, active and bored dogs tend to be destructive by unrolling toilet paper, chewing pillows, eating books, unravelling carpets and chewing furniture.

If your dog chews items like plants and furniture in your presence, it may be a form of attention-seeking behaviour. Dogs that are deeply distressed can wreak havoc by scratching and chewing their way out of or into homes and properties, often creating holes right through doors, tearing up flooring, breaking through windows and damaging steel security gates. These dogs are experiencing intense fear, which is usually associated with a specific fearful stimulus (noise phobia, for example), or with separation anxiety (see Chapter 9).

Digging

Digging is normal behaviour that easily becomes self-reinforcing: as the dog digs deeper, the soil, roots and insects provide a lot of interest. Reasons for digging include boredom, a need to bury or uncover a valuable object and temperature regulation (soil is a good insulator).

Make a digging patch for your dog, in a place you don't mind having dug up, by burying something smelly in the preferred spot. Make other areas less accessible and ensure your dog has one or more comfortable resting spots.

Below *Dogs usually find soil a comfortable surface to rest on.*

Chasing moving objects

Chasing bicycles, joggers and cars is self-reinforcing because it is always successful (whatever is chased does go away); hence the dog learns that chasing works. In order to re-teach this, a situation has to be set up repeatedly where chasing is not successful, i.e. the bicycle stops when the chasing starts and only moves again when the dog is under control. If your chasing canine tends to nip and grab as well, it is better to avoid these situations altogether and always ensure you have him on a lead in places where chasing may be triggered.

Barking

Barking could be attention-seeking behaviour as owners often inadvertently reinforce it, either because they feed or play with the dog, or verbally reprimand it. Barking can also inadvertently be reinforced when dogs bark at what they perceive to be a threat, such as a postman who, on retreating, gives the impression that their barking has been successful. You can re-teach dogs to be quiet in such instances by reinforcing quiet and substitute behaviour instead.

Right *This golden retriever is being rewarded for exercising self-control in the presence of a passing cyclist.*

Dogs that bark in their owners' absence may be doing so out of boredom or anxiety. Excessive vocalization is one of the symptoms of separation anxiety (see Chapter 9). Fear can cause barking, especially in novel situations (strange dogs, strange people). Don't reassure your dog that 'everything's fine' when it's not – you are simply reinforcing the fearfulness and therefore the barking.

Try to establish and remove the triggers for the barking, or remove the dog's access to them. This could mean preventing visual access to the neighbour's dogs or the front gate. If you need to confine your dog to decrease the barking, remember to increase his other forms of mental and physical stimulation. Night barkers often respond well to being kept indoors at night.

Above *Territorial barking at a fence is often reinforced because the passer-by seems to respond to the barking by going away. Teasing and shouting can also reinforce barking.*

Several commercial anti-barking devices are available. These are mounted on walls or counters, or attached to a neck collar, and activated when the dog barks. Devices that spray water or citronella oil or produce ultrasonic sound may be useful in managing excessive barking. Those that produce electric shocks are not recommended; shocks will worsen anxiety in anxious dogs. In any case, these devices do not always work because the underlying motivation for barking may be stronger than the negative stimulus from the device.

Jumping on countertops/stealing food/raiding the rubbish

You can re-teach dogs not to misbehave in your presence, but they will still do it when they are on their own. Make the problem places less attractive by using double-sided tape or make a booby-trap with a stack of cans. Taste aversion can be helpful – use a commercial pet deterrent.

The best way to deal with problems of this nature is through common sense – prevention is better than cure! Don't leave food out where your hungry Husky can get to it, for example, or put the rubbish down for a raiding Rottweiler.

Learn to live with it

Many dog behaviours are not acceptable to humans even though they are perfectly normal from the dog's point of view. Digging is normal for dogs, but frustrating for the gardening enthusiast. Sniffing crotches is normal for dogs, but embarrassing for the dinner host. It is easy to forget that dogs are animals, when we often treat them like humans.

If your dog's annoying habit is indeed normal for dogs – neither excessive nor dangerous for you or the dog – and represents an innate instinctive behaviour, you may need to accept that it is something you will have to live with and just manage as best you can. Be willing to compromise! Provide a digging patch for a keen digger, while making other areas less attractive for this activity. If your dog chases and kills cats, get used to the fact that you will not be able to acquire a cat for as long as you have the dog.

Above *Keep rubbish bins properly closed so that your dog doesn't learn bad habits. Each time she can successfully raid the rubbish, she is more likely to do so again.*

Chapter **9**

Behaviour therapy

Anxiety usually plays a role in more complex behavioural problems that do not respond to management solutions alone. In this chapter we look at aggression, fears and phobias, separation anxiety, compulsive behaviour and elimination disorders, and explore a practical approach to treating these problems. Of all these, aggression is the most common, and the most serious, dog behaviour problem.

Aggression

Canine aggression is by far the most common problem encountered by animal behaviourists. Dogs can inflict a lot of damage with their teeth (designed to do so), however dog bites and fights are very traumatic for all parties, especially if children are involved. The main causes of aggression are:

• Resource control
• Fear
• Frustration
• Pain
• Predatory instinct

A particular dog may be affected by one or more of these causes; the more specific the aggression, the easier it is to deal with it. With any form of aggression, you should avoid punishment completely, as it only escalates aggression. If a dog does show aggression,

withdraw whatever caused the aggression and confine the dog in an uninteresting place for a few minutes until it has cooled down. Ensure that the situation in which it showed aggression does not happen again while you put in place the skills and solutions needed to learn appropriate behaviour. Every time the dog can be aggressive successfully – namely, get rid of the perceived threat by using aggression – it learns to be better at being aggressive. Learned aggression can easily escalate to severe levels if you do nothing about it.

Household dogs

Fighting among dogs is a very common problem in multi-dog households. The most likely cause is resource control, as the dogs compete for access to resources. Pain can also cause aggression: a boisterous young puppy may inadvertently hurt an older, arthritic dog, inducing pain aggression. Redirected aggression often occurs at gates and fences, i.e. the dogs' aggressive behaviour is directed at something outside the gate, like a passing dog, and in the heat of the moment they attack each other. Interdog aggression is more common among dogs of the same gender and size. This is one

Opposite *Aggression is a serious problem, especially in a large breed dog, as those teeth can cause a lot of damage.*

reason it is not a good idea to get two puppies from the same litter, or two puppies of similar size, age and sex at the same time. Certain breeds are more inclined to fighting; terriers, and guard and defence dogs have a low interdog aggression threshold, and it doesn't take a lot for them to fight with other dogs.

Much interdog aggression only becomes evident when dogs reach social maturity, which is typically at two years of age, but this can range from one to three years. A typical situation is one where a dog that has given its owner no problems for two years will suddenly start fighting.

The dog that initiates the most interaction and controls the other dog(s) is likely to be the one with the higher status in terms of the inter-dog hierarchy. The dog that tends to back off and show submissive behaviour is naturally low in status. However, there is not always a clearly identifiable interdog hierarchy.

Dog fights usually happen in the presence of resources, in confined spaces, in areas where people spend a lot of time and when there is a high level of excitement, such as family home-comings. You should address or avoid such triggers. Among the ways to address interdog aggression are the following:

- Ensure the dogs recognize all the people in the household as effective resource managers (see Chapter 4). This will reduce competition among them.
- Address the interdog hierarchy: if there is a naturally more assertive individual, give him

Below *Two dogs of different size, sex and age are more likely to get along with each other.*

more privileges. This takes the pressure off the dog with the low status and reduces the tension. Ignore the less assertive dog in the other dog's presence – giving equal attention to every dog is not consistent with creating a secure social structure for dogs.

- If there is constant fighting, it is best to separate the dogs completely for a week or two while you institute better resource management. Do relaxation and self-control exercises with each dog before attempting a gradual, step-by-step reintroduction. Using muzzles or head collars is helpful during this process.

- Where dog fights become progressively worse and cause serious injury, it may be best to effect a permanent separation. This is best done by re-homing one of the dogs.

- Don't get involved in a dog fight yourself! If you have to break one up, rather use an object like a plank or broomstick. You could also throw a blanket over fighting dogs to startle them. It helps if both the dogs are wearing collars as it gives you something by which to grab the dog.

Strange dogs

All the different causes for aggression could play a role when dogs fight with unfamiliar dogs. The most common problem is fear due to a lack of socialization (see p125).

***Right** Apply all the rules of resource management in a household with more than one dog. Both dogs must be able to sit before they are given their food.*

Above If your dog does not allow you to attach the lead readily, it may be a sign of control-related aggression.

Familiar people

The typical form of aggression towards familiar people is a complex behaviour problem known as dominance aggression or control-related aggression. Dogs with control-related aggression are typically male and between 18 and 36 months of age (social maturity).

The typical presentation of control-related aggression is that of a beloved family dog who suddenly turns on one (or more) family members. The aggression is often elicited by certain actions towards the dog, such as:

- Staring
- Patting on the head
- Hugging
- Kissing
- Putting on a lead or collar
- Handling the head or muzzle
- Stepping over it
- Pushing it out of the way or off a couch
- Verbally reprimanding it
- Correcting it with a lead
- Punishing it
- Disturbing its sleep
- Removing an object over which it has control

The issue is control of physical and social resources. The dog wants to control his own resources and reacts with aggression when he perceives them under threat (the threat may not be real or intended).

Such dogs are usually anxious about their social structure. They feel insecure and use aggression to test their status in the social system. They can be very demanding of attention at times, but randomly and unpredictably respond aggressively when people initiate interaction. They may control people's access to certain areas – for example, by not allowing a husband to get into bed with his wife – control tug games and toys and may often lean on or straddle people, put their paws on their shoulders, stare at them and growl when they are handled.

These dogs appear to have difficulty relating properly to people in terms of social status. They need very decisive leadership and to see people as highly effective resource managers, not threats. The dog must learn that there is no need for him to control any resources. Pay attention to the following:

- Avoid all situations in which aggression is likely to take place. Never punish aggression.
- You must take resource management seriously. The dog should only ever obtain access to a resource if it defers to humans – complies with an instruction. That means the dog must always sit when asked to sit, and lie down or wait before he either gets fed, gets attention, goes for a walk or before you play with him.
- You must stoically ignore all your dog's attempts to initiate interaction.
- Although predictability and routine are important for dogs generally, these dogs often perceive the predictability of their environment as a way in which they can

Above *Dogs with control-related aggression should be expected to sit for anything they consider valuable, such as attention and food, at all times.*

control it. When they expect to be fed, they are. When they expect to be let out, they are. This is simply because they have become used to it. In these cases, being slightly unpredictable will reinforce your dog's dependence on you for access to resources. Feed at a different time or even skip a meal once in a while and change his walk and play schedule slightly.
- Reintroduce the triggers for aggression gradually, in controlled circumstances, once you have reinstated resource control and rule structure. In some cases, medication needs to be prescribed.

If you are scared of your dog or if it has already bitten someone you should immediately get the help of a qualified animal behaviourist or veterinarian.

> *Nothing in life is free for a dog with control-related aggression*

Strange people

Aggression towards strangers is, in most cases, the product of fear. Either you have not adequately socialized your dog or he has had a negative, fearful experience with unfamiliar people. Systematic desensitization and counter-conditioning is very successful in these cases, provided treatment starts as soon as possible after the problem becomes apparent (see p120).

Other animals

Predatory aggression towards small animals, due to the highly instinctive nature of this behaviour, is very difficult to treat successfully. Dogs with a high predatory instinct should be kept on leads when a risk exists for such aggression and should be kept in a home where there are no small, prey-like pets.

Above Thunderstorm phobia can cause intense distress that manifests as destructive behaviour. This dog's phobia, characterised by scratching the wall, was intensified whenever she was alone during a thunderstorm.

Fears and phobias

Fear is normal – very often it can be life-saving. However, when an animal does not get used to whatever is causing the fear, it becomes a problem. Phobias are very intense, abnormal fears. Fears develop gradually, while phobias develop suddenly and animals do not get used to what is causing them.

Phobic dogs hyperventilate, shiver and try to run away or hide from the source of the perceived threat. They show intensely fearful body language and may even urinate, defaecate and empty the contents of their anal sacs.

Treatment involves desensitization, counter-conditioning and medication (see p182). Noise-phobic dogs benefit from access to a safe, preferably soundproof 'den' where they can hide when they become phobic. Be careful not to reinforce a phobic dog's fear by comforting it too much during such an event – too much attention could be rewarding and may increase the fear. Just be there for your dog without fussing too much over it. Talk to your vet about medication and the use of canine pheromone products.

Compulsive behaviour

Compulsive behaviour refers to out-of-context, repetitive behaviour, that is difficult or impossible to interrupt. When any normal behaviour, such as licking or barking, is suddenly performed so excessively that it interferes with the dog's normal functioning, it becomes compulsive. Examples of compulsive behaviour are:

- Tail-chasing
- Fly-biting
- Shadow-chasing
- Constant licking of the skin (acral lick granuloma)
- Constant ingestion of stones or other non-food items
- Constant barking
- Constant licking; for example, walls or floors

There certainly appears to be a breed predisposition in some cases, such as in the case of tail-chasing in white bull terriers. Stress and anxiety also play a role, but the underlying pathology is not well understood. Inadvertently

Above *Tail chasing can be a compulsive disorder if it occurs excessively and interferes with the dog's normal daily activities and functions.*

reinforcing such behaviour by paying it attention can also play a role in its development into a compulsion.

Try to· recognize the triggers for compulsive behaviour and eliminate them or interrupt the behaviour and redirect it to something functional and acceptable. This, together with environmental enrichment and medication, can be used to treat these dogs.

Separation anxiety

Dogs with separation anxiety are destructive in the absence of their owners. They are typically over-attached to them, become anxious before they leave and show very exuberant greeting behaviour when their owners return home and follow them everywhere. These dogs are unable to cope with being alone. They may also bark or howl excessively, urinate and defaecate in inappropriate places, pace up and down and drool with saliva when alone.

The distress usually starts within 30 minutes of the departure of the owner, and pretty much continues until he or she returns. Not all dogs that are destructive in the owner's absence suffer from classical separation anxiety. Sometimes a dog that is not over-attached to his owner has a bad experience at home alone. He associates the bad experience (for example, a severe thunderstorm) with the owner's absence and thereafter becomes anxious about the owner leaving – even when there is no storm. Dogs can also experience separation distress when something familiar in the environment changes, for example when you move to a new home or replace their kennel. If a dog is destructive only on some days and not continuously, it may simply be that it is overactive and bored.

Left *Treating separation anxiety: reduce the stress associated with departures by pretending that you are leaving when you are not.*

Follow these guidelines on how to treat separation anxiety:

- Encourage independent behaviour; for example, by creating opportunities for play with a toy a short distance away rather than right next to you.
- Reduce attention-seeking behaviour (see p163).
- Keep arrivals and departures low-key by not getting excited or making a fuss. Ignore the dog for at least half an hour before leaving.
- Desensitize the dog to departure cues by associating them with things other than departures. Pick up the car keys when you are not about to leave and exit through a different door when you do leave.
- Desensitize the dog to your absence by practising the 'steady stay' described in Chapter 6 and spend incrementally more time out of sight. Close doors between you and your dog when you are at home for short periods at first, gradually increasing the time duration.
- When your dog has to be left alone, try to keep the environment as much as possible like it is when you are home. For example, leave the radio on (if that is what you normally do when you are home), leave an article of clothing with your scent on it with the dog and allow her access to a room or area where you spend a lot of time together.
- Discuss the possibility of medication with your veterinarian.

Right Leave a separation-anxious dog with familiar scents and sounds when she has to be alone. Her owner's scarf and the radio help this dog relax.

Inappropriate elimination

Possible reasons for messing in the house include the following:

- Incomplete house-training.
- Medical problems; for example, urinary incontinence.
- Insufficient access to a preferred spot.
- Separation anxiety (only in the absence of the owner).
- Attention-seeking behaviour (only in the presence of the owner).
- Submissive urination – usually in young puppies and during greetings.
- Excitement urination.
- Intense fear.
- Marking behaviour.
- Old age – part of canine cognitive dysfunction syndrome (canine Alzheimer's).

A dog that has not been properly house-trained will have to be taught from scratch where to eliminate by means of constant supervision, frequent access to the preferred spot and immediate reward the instant it does eliminate in the correct place (wait for it to finish first). Ensure your dog does not associate the place you designate for elimination with anything negative, such as punishment or fear.

A dog that was properly house-trained at some stage in its life and suddenly starts urinating and/or defaecating in the house may have a medical problem.

Marking behaviour occurs in both male and female dogs, but is most common in intact males. Castration is recommended. Urine

Above *Male dogs typically urinate against vertical objects. When this occurs inside the home, it is often a sign of social anxiety.*

marking occurs in response to social change in the household, such as a new boyfriend or pet. Unforced, positive interaction with the newcomer should address the problem.

Approach a dog with submissive urination in a completely non-threatening manner by keeping your body low. At first, don't even approach the dog, but wait for him to approach you. Avoid direct eye contact and do not lean over him. Reward your dog with a treat if he doesn't urinate.

A systematic approach to behavioural problems

A systematic approach to a behaviour problem is more likely to be successful than a quick-fix approach (see p185). It should be instituted in planned phases:

- Prepare a clean slate – remove the triggers
- Eliminate the physical causes
- Put the necessary skills and solutions in place
- Reintroduce the triggers

Last-resort options include re-homing and euthanasia.

Start with a clean slate

It is always best if you can completely avoid triggers of the problem behaviour when you

Above Remove access to the trigger: If the dog dislikes small children, put the dog away when the children come to visit.

commence the behaviour therapy programme. The best way to do this is to temporarily remove those stimuli that cause the problem; once you have properly addressed the underlying issues, you can reintroduce the triggers under controlled circumstances.

Remove access to triggers

If you cannot remove the trigger, try removing the dog from the trigger. With a dog that is fearful of children, for example, keep the dog away from children.

Eliminate physical causes

Behavioural symptoms can be caused by physical conditions, such as infectious diseases; worm infestations; poisoning; pain, as in the case of arthritis and ear infections; thyroid disease; poor eyesight and hearing; bladder problems; and nutritional disorders. Have your veterinarian check your dog out before you decide that it has a primary behaviour problem. First treat all the physical conditions before continuing with behaviour therapy.

The effect of hormones

The reproductive hormones can affect a dog's behaviour. Spaying (surgical removal of the ovaries and uterus in the female dog) and castration (surgical removal of the testicles in the male dog) can also have behavioural effects.

The effects of castration include the following:
• Reduced intensity of aggression.
• Lower threshold for aggression – it takes more to trigger aggression.

Below *An uncastrated male dog (left). When male dogs are castrated, the scrotum (contains the testicles) becomes smaller. There are no external signs confirming that a female has been spayed. This female (right) is not showing signs of being on heat.*

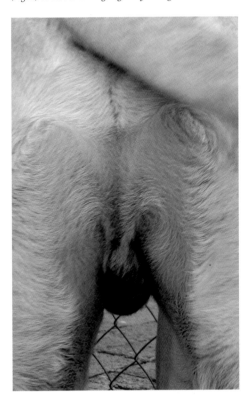 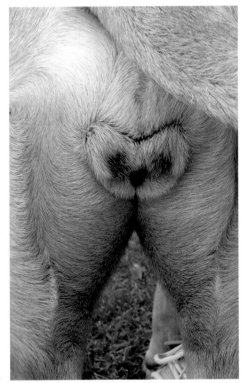

- Reduction in roaming behaviour.
- Reduction in urine-marking behaviour.
- Reduction in mounting behaviour.

Spaying results in:
- Absence of heat cycles.
- Inability to fall pregnant.
- Reduced fighting among bitches.

Both spaying and castration reduce interdog aggression. In male dogs, if there is a clearly defined interdog hierarchy, it makes sense to castrate only the individual with the lower status in order to increase the difference in social status between the two dogs. However, even if all of the dogs are castrated the fighting should lessen, as the intensity of aggression will have been reduced.

Skills and solutions

Teach your dog social skills and provide it with an environment wherein it is able to behave appropriately. This includes one or more of:
- Establishing a clear social structure (see Chapter 4)
- Establishing a clear rule structure (see Chapter 4)
- Teaching relaxation skills and self-control (see Chapter 6)
- Teaching a substitute behaviour (see Chapter 8)

Restart/reintroduce triggers

Reintroduce triggers (if you cannot permanently eliminate them) in controlled circumstances. Use relaxation and self-control skills to enhance appropriate behaviour.

Above Reintroduce the triggers: once a clear social and rule structure has been established, the dog is introduced to young children, with whom she was previously uncomfortable, in a controlled and pleasant manner.

Systematic desensitization and counter-conditioning

Counter-conditioning is a form of classical conditioning and comprises changing the effects of an earlier conditioning experience by, for example, playing with a dog during a thunderstorm so that it learns to associate thunderstorms with fun instead of fear. Systematic desensitization is a specific type of counter-conditioning that teaches the animal to relax in the presence of a fear-evoking stimulus such as in the case of teaching a gun-shy dog to tolerate gunshots.

Systematic desensitization refers to gradual, controlled exposure to triggers that cause fear or aggression. The trigger is introduced at an intensity that doesn't elicit the undesired response. The dog is then taught to associate the mild form of the trigger with pleasant emotions elicited by for example food or play,

essentially replacing the negative emotion with a positive response. Then the intensity of the trigger is gradually increased, still associated with pleasant experiences. Because the level of the negative stimulus is increased in tiny increments, the dog habituates (gets used) to it. Eventually, the dog can cope with the initially stressful stimulus.

Two things determine the success of a desensitization programme: firstly, you need to identify your dog's tolerance threshold to the stimulus that causes the problem. In other words, how loud must gunshots be before they frighten your dog? Where on the body can you touch the aggressive dog without eliciting an inappropriate response? Once you have determined this level, you can start with the desensitization process.

Secondly, you must be able to increase the intensity of the stimulus in very small steps.

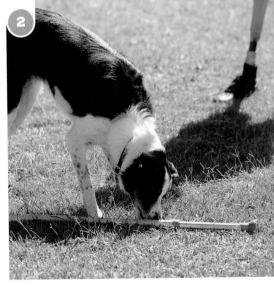

During the desensitization programme, it is important that you do not expose your dog to the full stimulus as this may cause the problem to regress. If at any stage during the process your dog reacts to the stimulus with fear or aggression, reduce its intensity to a level your dog can handle and proceed slowly with gradual increases in the stimulus.

A desensitization programme may take minutes or months to complete. Work in daily sessions of about 20 minutes, or twice daily for 10–15 minutes. You can use training in conjunction with desensitization by teaching your dog to perform behaviours on cue in the presence of the fearful stimulus, for rewards. Ask your dog to sit, and reward him. Ask him to lie down and reward him. Give a paw and reward, and so on. This helps because it gives the dog something active to do instead of being scared.

1 The border collie is fearful of the walking stick.
2 When the stick is flat on the ground, it doesn't cause fear. This is the starting point for the desensitization process.
3 In many tiny steps, the stick is gradually lifted off the ground. Each time the dog receives a reward (a click and treat in this case) when she approaches and sniffs the stick without showing fear.
4 At the end of the desensitization programme, the dog is comfortable walking right next to the stick.

Last-resort options

Re-homing

Rehoming a dog with a behaviour problem is justified when your dog is exhibiting behaviour that is normal, but not suitable for the environment she is in. One such example is when a dog with a strong herding instinct exhibits compulsive circling because she is living in an apartment.

Euthanasia

For some people, euthanasia is an easy way out of having to deal with a problem dog. For others, it is the most difficult decision of their lives. Euthanasia should never be a standard recommendation for aggression towards people, for example. Each case should be judged on its own merits. Sometimes, it is indeed the best option, especially when the problem behaviour poses a serious threat to people's safety or when the dog is experiencing severe anxiety that is resistant to behaviour therapy.

The use of medication to treat behaviour problems

Some behaviour problems respond well to medication such as anti-anxiety drugs and anti-depressants. However, not all behavioural conditions respond to medication, so you need to rely on your veterinarian to prescribe the medication for your dog's particular case. The vet will base the prescription on a thorough assessment, and carefully monitor the treatment. Some drugs take several weeks to take effect.

Below When dogs and people are well matched, behaviour problems are less likely to occur. Small dogs with low reactivity levels are easily managed by the older dog owner, and at the same time provide valuabe companionship.

Realistic expectations: cure vs control

With many behaviour problems, it is not realistic to expect a complete cure. You may never cure control-related aggression, for example, but you can control it effectively. This requires ongoing application of behaviour therapy. Realistically, when you live with a dog with a serious behaviour problem, you can expect to achieve an acceptable level of control over it, but you should always be aware that it could crop up again.

Treat the cause, not the symptom

When you have a dog with a behaviour problem, the problem you see is usually only a symptom of a larger underlying issue. Aggression could be a symptom of an underlying anxiety related to the dog's perception of his social structure, or a symptom of inappropriate punishment. He could be manifesting compulsive behaviour because of an inability to

Above Ensure that your lifestyle allows you to satisfy all your dog's mental and physical needs. This will help prevent behaviour problems.

cope with stress, or be destructive as the result of separation anxiety, boredom or attention-seeking behaviour.

Quick-fix, symptomatic solutions are unlikely to significantly sustain an improvement in behaviour, and often do not enhance the dog's quality of life. A thorough approach is more likely to lead to successful resolution of a behaviour problem. Address the underlying issue by ensuring that your dog's basic needs are all fulfilled properly: establish a healthy social structure and a clear rule structure, provide adequate and appropriate mental and physical stimulation, and an enriched environment. Above all, be committed to the wellbeing of your dog and value the companionship he or she offers.

Glossary

Acral lick granuloma – ulcerative skin lesion on the lower legs caused by incessant licking.

Anal sac – a small glandular structure under the skin located on either side of the anus, opening into the anus via small ducts.

Attention-seeking behaviour – dog behaviour to elicit social interaction.

Bite inhibition – the ability to control the intensity of a bite, i.e. not biting hard.

Body harness – a harness that fits around the dog's chest as an alternative to a neck collar.

Calming signals – subtle body language used by a dog during interaction with another dog in order to calm the other animal.

Capturing a behaviour – marking and rewarding behaviour that occurs spontaneously and without any help through luring or coercion.

Castration – a surgical procedure to remove the testicles of a dog.

Classical conditioning – helping a dog to form associations between two events that were initially not connected with one another.

Clicker training – an animal training method that makes use of the sound of the clicker as a conditioned positive reinforcer.

Compulsive behaviour – repetitive behaviour of a dog, in excess of that required for normal functioning and therefore interfering with the dog's normal functioning.

Cue – a signal (verbal or visual) given to an animal to elicit a certain behaviour.

Deference – voluntary and respectful yielding of privileges to a higher ranking individual,

Desensitization – gradual exposure to a stimulus to reduce a dog's reaction to the stimulus.

Dysplasia (also hip/elbow dysplasia) – abnormal development of the hip joint resulting in looseness of the joint, causing pain and, in the long term, arthritis.

Distance-decreasing signals – body language used by a dog to appease another dog, i.e. showing willingness to interact.

Distance-increasing signals – body language used by a dog to keep distance between he or she and another dog, i.e. warning the other individual not to come too close.

Dog-appeasing pheromone (DAP) – chemical substance released by lactating bitches that causes dogs to relax. It is now produced synthetically to help in the treatment of anxieties, fears and phobias.

Euthanasia – humane killing of animals, usually by lethal injection.

Extinction – permanent removal of a reward for a certain behaviour, which results in the behaviour not occurring anymore.

Fly-biting – a dog biting at real or imaginary flies, often a compulsive action.

Food-dispensing toys – toys that can be filled with dog food that is released, through various mechanisms, when the dog plays with the toy.

Gundogs – dogs that were originally bred to accompany bird hunters, and used either to point out location of the prey, flush it out from the undergrowth, or mark and retrieve shot birds (e.g. pointers, setters, retrievers).

Habituation – getting used to a new stimulus by repeated exposure.

Head collar – specially designed collar that fits around the dog's head in a manner similar to a horse's halter, as an alternative for a neck collar (not to be confused with a muzzle).

Heelwork – teaching a dog to walk at heel, i.e. right next to the handler without pulling in front or lagging behind.

Herding dogs – dogs that were originally bred to herd sheep and other flock animals.

Hypersalivation – drooling.

Hyperventilation – fast breathing, panting.

Interdog aggression – fighting between dogs.

Lure – using a treat to lead the dog through a certain behaviour (also the actual treat or toy).

Mouthing – holding objects, including people's limbs, in the mouth without biting.

Operant conditioning – a dog learning to do something because it will have a positive consequence, or to avoid a negative consequence.

Muzzle – restraint to prevent dogs from biting.

Pheromones – chemical substances secreted by animals from various parts of the body, e.g. urine, faeces and skin glands, to communicate via smell with others of the same species.

Play bow – body posture that usually precedes play (chest on the ground, hindquarters up).

Resource control – controlling the dog's access to things that it considers to be of value.

Scent hounds – dogs originally bred to assist in the hunt by following the scent of prey (e.g. Bloodhounds, Beagle, Basset Hound).

Scruffing – grabbing an animal by the skin on top of the neck, and shaking it.

Send-away – sending a dog away from the handler, i.e. the dog moves away in a certain direction on instruction from the handler.

Separation anxiety – a condition exhibited by dogs who don't cope with being alone; severe anxiety usually manifests in destructiveness, vocalisation, or messing of urine and faeces.

Shadow-chasing – chasing the movement caused by the interplay of light and shade on a surface such as a floor, or wall.

Shaping – reinforcing better versions of behaviour until a polished version has been learnt.

Sight hounds – dogs originally bred to hunt by picking up the movement of prey and then chasing it down (e.g. Borzoi, Saluki, Afghan).

Sit-stay – sitting and remaining in that position while the handler walks out of sight, and in the presence of distractions.

Socialization – getting used to interacting with other creatures (dogs, people, other animals).

Spaying – surgical procedure to remove the uterus and ovaries of a bitch.

Tail-chasing – compulsive behaviour of a dog continually chasing its own tail.

Target stick – stick or pointer used to teach the dog to touch objects with its nose.

Tug games – playing with tug toys, i.e. the dog pulls at the one end and the owner at the other end, or two dogs play with each other.

Urine marking – urinating in certain places to mark territory.

Contacts & further reading

Further reading

Breeds

Coile, Dr Caroline. *Encyclopedia of Dog Breeds* (2005). Hauppauge, New York: Barron's Educational Series Inc.

Cunliffe, Juliette. *The Encyclopedia of Dog Breeds* (2005). Bath: Parragon.

Fogle, Dr B. *Dogalog* (2002). London: Dorling Kindersley Publishing.

Fogle, Dr B. *The New Encyclopedia of the Dog* (2000). London: Dorling Kindersley Publishing.

General behaviour and training

Burch, Mary R. and Bailey, Jon S. *How Dogs Learn* (1999). Hoboken NJ: Wiley Publishers (Howell Book House).

Donaldson, Jean. *The Culture Clash* (1996). James & Kenneth Publishers.

Pryor, Karen. *Don't Shoot the Dog! The New Art of Teaching and Training* (2002). Ringpress Books Ltd.

Abrantes, Roger. *Dog Language: An Encyclopedia of Canine Behaviour* (2001). Wenatchee WA: Dogwise Publishing.

Aloff, Brenda. *Positive Reinforcement: Training Dogs in the Real World* (2001). Neptune City, New Jersey: T.F.H. Publications.

Clicker Training

Books

Alexander, M.C. *Click for Joy! Questions and Answers from Clicker Trainers and their Dogs* (2003). Waltham (USA): Sunshine Books Inc.

Laurence, Kay. *Clicker Foundation Training*; *Clicker Novice Training*; *Clicker Intermediate Training*; *Clicker World Obedience Training*. Learning about Dogs, available via website (www.learningaboutdogs.com).

Pryor, Karen. *Clicker training for dogs* (2005). Waltham (USA): Sunshine Books Inc.

Videos

Clicker Clips. Kay Laurence, Learning About Dogs.

Clicker Clips Intermediate. Kay Laurence, Learning About Dogs.
PO Box 13, Chipping Campden
Glos. GL5 6WX
United Kingdom
www.learningaboutdogs.com

Clicker Training with Dr Quixi. EduPet.
  PO Box 100689
  Moreleta Plaza
  South Africa 0167
  email: edupetmail@mweb.co.za
  www.edupet.co.za

Websites on clicker training
www.clickertraining.com
www.learningaboutdogs.com
www.clickersolutions.com

Toys and equipment

Treat-dispensing toys for dogs
www.bustercube.com
www.sitstay.com

Leads and harnesses
www.realdog.co.nz
www.petfooddirect.com

Kong toys
www.kongcompany.com

Associations

United States
American Pet Association
PO Box 7172 Boulder, CO 80306-7172
tel: Main 800-APA-PETS (800-272-7387)
email: apa@apapets.org
www.apapets.com

Association of Pet Dog Trainers
PO Box 3734, Salinas, CA 93912-3734
tel: (408) 663 9257; 1(800) PET-DOGS
www.apdt.com

United Kingdom
Federation of Dog Trainers and Canine
  Behaviourists
15 Lightburne Avenue
Lytham St Annes, Lancs, FY8 1JE
email: gen@fdtcb.com
www.fdtcb.com

The Association of Pet Behaviour Counsellors
PO Box 46, Worcester, WR8 9YS
tel: 01386 751151
email: apbc@petbcent.demon.co.uk
www.apbc.org.uk

Index

Acknowledgements

This book is dedicated to my late parents, Konrad and Annegret Sonntag, whose love, support and encouragement enabled me to pursue my dreams.

My sincere appreciation to all those who have helped me directly or indirectly, to complete this project. Friends, family, staff, colleagues, professional publishing people, clients, patients and pets all played a role and deserve a huge thank you! Wags and hugs especially to all the canine and human models who sacrificed time and patience to help produce the lovely pictures in the book.

A special thanks to Brian de Kock and Cathy van Zyl of Diocesan College, Rondebosch, for usage of the grounds for the duration of shoot/main location etc.

Trainers and Dogs:
Marizelle, and cross-Staffordshire Terrier Rexie, Belgian Shepherd Nikita, cross-Italian Greyhound Roxy and Fox Terrier Jenny; Marycke, and Golden Retreivers Jenna and Lola; Elna, and German Shepherds Duke and Nizza; Candice, and Golden Retreiver Xena; Dudley, and Great Dane Keera; Stephanie, and German Shepherd Moya; Jean, and Border Collies Gemma and Leea; Di, and Australian Shepherd Moya, Bearded Collies Kianga & Tshebe; Jenny, and German Shepherd Mango; Ryno, and Bouviers Garbo and Narla, and Fox Terrier Mia; Janet, and Border Collie Treat; Keely and Mira, and Bullmastiff Maya.

Photography

All photography by Ryno for New Holland Image Library (NHIL), with the exception of the following photographers and/or their agencies. Copyright rests with these individuals and/or their agencies:

Front cover, NHIL/Ryno; p13, Gallo Images; p14, Gallo Images; p174, Magdie van Heerden; p180, Quixi Sonntag; p184, NHIL/Dorothée von der Osten.